92774
4. 5. 78

£5.95

BIRMINGHAM UNIVERSITY LIBRARY

~ S BOOK MUST BE RETURNED
~ DIATELY IF RECALLED FOR
~ NOTHER BORROWER,
OR BEFORE THE

D1356772

THE SOCIALIST DECISION

PAUL TILLICH

The Socialist Decision

Translated by Franklin Sherman

HARPER & ROW, PUBLISHERS
NEW YORK, HAGERSTOWN,
SAN FRANCISCO, LONDON

1817

Translated from the German, *Die sozialistische Entscheidung*, as published in Paul Tillich, *Gesammelte Werke*, vol. 2, *Frühe Schriften zum Religiösen Sozialismus* (Evangelisches Verlag, Stuttgart, 1962). The original edition was published by Alfred Protte, Potsdam, 1933.

THE SOCIALIST DECISION. Copyright © 1977 by Harper & Row, Publishers, Inc. All rights reserved. Printed in the United States of America. No part of this book may be used or reproduced in any manner whatsoever without written permission except in the case of brief quotations embodied in critical articles and reviews. For information address Harper & Row, Publishers, Inc., 10 East 53rd Street, New York, N.Y. 10022. Published simultaneously in Canada by Fitzhenry & Whiteside Limited, Toronto.

FIRST EDITION

Designed by Sidney Feinberg

Library of Congress Cataloging in Publication Data

Tillich, Paul, 1886–1965.
　The socialist decision.
　Translation of Die sozialistische Entscheidung.
　Includes bibliographical references and index.
　1. Socialism. I. Title.
HX56.T5313　1977　　335　　76–62928
ISBN 0–06–068252–3

1075721

77 78 79 80 81 10 9 8 7 6 5 4 3 2 1

Contents

PART TWO: THE PRINCIPLE OF BOURGEOIS SOCIETY AND THE INNER CONFLICT OF SOCIALISM

3. The Bourgeois Principle and the Proletariat

4. The Inner Conflict of Socialism

PART THREE: THE PRINCIPLE OF SOCIALISM AND THE SOLUTION OF ITS INNER CONFLICT

5. The Socialist Principle and its Roots

Introduction by John R. Stumme

The original edition of this book, Paul Tillich's most extensive work on social and political questions, was published in Germany early in the fateful year 1933, just as Adolf Hitler was coming to power. As Tillich explains in the opening paragraphs, it is both a call to the German public to consider the socialist alternative in the political and economic crises that were besetting it, and a call to socialists themselves to reconsider the deepest roots of their beliefs.

The Socialist Decision represents the culmination of nearly fifteen years' intense preoccupation by the early Tillich with the question of "religious socialism." Those who know Tillich only from his later writings in America are largely unaware of this dimension of his thought, since he turned later chiefly to psychological, ontological, and theological themes. A major portion of his earlier career, however, was devoted to the development of social theory. In his 1936 autobiographical sketch "On the Boundary," Tillich refers to his living "on the boundary between Lutheranism and socialism."[1] The tension that these alternatives imply between the religious and the political, between pessimism

1. *On the Boundary: An Autobiographical Sketch* (New York: Scribner's, 1966), pp. 74–81. This is a revised translation of the essay that appeared as part one of Tillich's *The Interpretation of History* (New York: Scribner's, 1936).

and utopianism, conservatism and radicalism, is amply illustrated in the present volume.

The historical roots of the problem lay in the chasm that had developed in the nineteenth century between the emerging industrial proletariat and the Protestant churches. The year 1848, a year of revolution, marked the decisive break. In that year Karl Marx and Friedrich Engels gave the proletariat its revolutionary charter in the *Communist Manifesto*, and at Wittenberg, over the grave of Martin Luther, J. H. Wichern replied with a counterrevolutionary "Protestant Manifesto." Wichern succeeded in making "Inner Mission" the major ecclesiastical answer to the new problems of industrialization, but his program of charitable works was a very weak response to the smoldering discontent of the proletariat. "After 1848," writes William O. Shanahan, "German Protestantism gradually lost its power to reach and stir the masses: their world and their life became increasingly alien."[2] The church became the ally of Prussian conservatism, supporting monarchial and authoritarian institutions and opposing democratic and social policies.

Meanwhile the urban proletariat found in an anticlerical, Marxist-shaped socialism its source of hope and power. Ferdinand Lassalle began the German labor movement in 1863 and in spite of Bismarck's Anti-Socialist Law of 1878, the Social Democratic party grew rapidly. Engels and Karl Kautsky, building on the work of Marx, provided the movement with its orthodox ideology, an ideology that either rejected religion entirely or, at best, restricted it to the private sphere. (This orthodoxy still prevailed in 1932 among what Tillich calls in this book "the older generation of socialists.") Both sides considered it a truism that "Christianity and socialism are opposed like fire and water" (August Bebel).

The son of a Lutheran parsonage in a small, walled, feudallike town in east-Elbian Prussia, the young Paul Tillich absorbed the religious and political views of his environment. Born in 1886,

2. *German Protestants Face the Social Question*, vol. 1, *The Conservative Phase: 1815–1871* (Notre Dame, Indiana: University of Notre Dame Press, 1954), p. 193.

three years after the death of Marx and at a time when the socialist party was proscribed, he learned that socialism was "revolutionary, which meant criminal."[3] His move to Berlin in 1900 and his later theological and philosophical education in Berlin, Tübingen, and Halle broadened his horizons, but did not fundamentally alter his social and political attitudes. He remained indifferent to politics, which in fact meant the acceptance of his church's conservative, nationalistic, and quietistic teachings. Shortly after the beginning of war in August 1914, Tillich, loyal to throne and altar, volunteered to serve as a chaplain in the German Imperial Army.

Tillich was initially an enthusiastic supporter of the war. His first reports to his superiors from his position on the Western front were those of a willing officer, confidently and conscientiously performing his duty. Before long, however, the serious problematic of the war became evident. The war that was to have been won in a matter of months kept dragging on and on. The experience of having to bury his officer friends and to officiate at mass burials of the troops, the horrors of combat, and the constant presence of death created a crisis in his own life. In a report in 1915 he spoke of "being broken within," and in a private letter in 1916 he wrote of "living through the actual world destruction of this time."[4] Later he referred to his war experience as marking a "personal *kairos*" in his own life.[5]

Tillich's early world was gone forever; there was no going home. Through the war he came in direct contact with the proletariat for the first time and discovered something of its plight and bitterness. His eyes were opened to the sharp split between the classes, to the sociological limits of the church, and to the demonic power of militarism, nationalism, and capitalism.

3. "Autobiographical Reflections," in Charles W. Kegley and Robert W. Bretall, eds., *The Theology of Paul Tillich* (New York: Macmillan, 1952), p. 7.

4. "Bericht über die Monate November und Dezember 1915," *Gesammelte Werke*, vol. 13 (Stuttgart: Evangelisches Verlagswerk, 1972), p. 78. Letter to Maria Rhine, 27 November, 1916, p. 70.

5. D. Mackenzie Brown, ed., *Ultimate Concern: Tillich in Dialogue*, (New York: Harper & Row, 1965), p. 153.

After four traumatic years on the front lines, Tillich returned to a defeated Germany convinced that the old order was irretrievably destroyed.

He was not in Berlin long before a violent uprising swept through the capital city. The sudden, brief November Revolution of 1918 dethroned the kaiser and initiated a democratic republic in which the Social Democrats, who until now had always been in opposition, were the predominant power. For the first time Tillich became alive to the political situation, responding positively to the turn of events. The reaction of the church was predictable. The loss of the emperor, the supreme bishop of the church; the separation of church and state; and the political gains of their enemies shocked the church authorities. They resented their losses, longed for the past and obstructed the way of the few socialists in their midst.

Tillich, however, could no longer accept his church's political views. He recognized the need for a new religious social philosophy, one that took seriously the realities of the proletarian situation. And seeing in socialism the best resources for dealing with these realities and in constructing a new social order, Tillich made his own "socialist decision." The unlikely candidate, Paul Tillich, doctor of philosophy, Prussian Evangelical pastor, chaplain in the kaiser's army, became a socialist. In a pamphlet written at this time, Tillich urged "representatives of Christianity and the church who stand on socialist soil to enter into the socialist movement in order to pave the way for a future union of Christianity and the socialist social order." Tillich himself set out to follow what he then called "this difficult, unknown, important way."[6]

The crisis of war and revolution soon came to represent for Tillich a decisive turning point in the history of Germany and Europe. Perceiving the present moment in epochal terms, he envisioned a qualitatively new beginning arising from the rubble of defeat and chaos. "Will not a third period of Christianity beyond

6. "Der Sozialismus als Kirchenfrage," *GW*, 2 (1962), p. 19. This is a pamphlet coauthored by Tillich and Carl Richard Wegener, and first published in 1919.

Catholicism and Protestantism arise? Is not this the meaning of the 'turning of the world' [*Weltenwende*] which the world war and the revolution have brought us?" he asked rhetorically.[7] And in his first essay on socialism (the pamphlet already referred to), he wrote:

> We stand in a period of dissolution. A new age of unity is arising. Socialism will form its economic and social foundation. And Christianity stands before the task to convey to this development its moral and religious powers and thereby to initiate a great new synthesis of religion and social structure.[8]

Grasped by the consciousness of a *kairos*, a moment rich in significance, Tillich intuited the beginning of a new age where the static opposition of socialism and religion would give way to a new synthesis characterized by economic justice and an awareness of the presence of the divine in everything human.

Tillich's concern with religion and socialism thus was far more than a question of how the workers could be won back to participation in ecclesiastical institutions. Neither did he see the primary issue as that of personal allegiance, that is, whether or not it was possible to be both a Christian and a socialist. Nor was Tillich's religious socialism a veiled attempt to win the workers away from the socialist parties and philosophy for a conservative, religiously sponsored political program, or an effort to cover over the class divisions of society with the soft words of religion. Tillich's religious socialism was none of these, though others used the same label to pursue these ends. Rather his luring, encompassing vision of a new society drove him to probe the elemental roots of both socialism and Christianity and from there to criticize and to transform them both.

Soon after the November Revolution Tillich sought out other Christians who supported the revolution and endorsed socialism. The number of such people in socialist Berlin and, indeed, in all of Germany, was not large. Prior to the war no religious socialist

---

7. "Revolution und Kirche," *GW*, 12 (1971), p. 199. A review of an anthology of the same name, first published in *Das Neue Deutschland*, 1919.
8. "Der Sozialismus als Kirchenfrage," p. 16.

movement had existed in Germany. Christoph Blumhardt's affirmation of socialism in Württemberg at the turn of the century had had little direct impact on the German churches, although it had influenced Hermann Kutter and Leonhard Ragaz to begin a religious socialist movement in Switzerland. In Germany itself, religious socialism was a postwar phenomenon. Called forth by the revolution, it began and continued as a marginal, radical movement on the edge of the church's life.

Tillich found his initial conversational partners in a small group that had been instigated by Siegmund-Schultze's *Soziale Arbeitsgemeinschaft*, a settlement house-type organization in east Berlin. This modest, unassuming gathering, composed principally of clergy, met weekly during 1919. Here Tillich forged his friendship and working alliance with another pastor, Carl Mennicke, and gradually the two formed their own circle of religious socialists.

Tillich began his teaching career in the spring term of 1919 at the University of Berlin with a lecture course significantly entitled "Christianity and the Present Social Problem." From this time onwards, he pursued his political activities from the locus of a university, first at Berlin, then at Marburg, Dresden, Leipzig, and finally Frankfurt. Tillich was not very successful in personally overcoming the distance between professor and proletariat or that between intellectual and party. He did, however, consider his affirmation of socialism as a support, directly or indirectly, of the socialist parties. And he did come to know personally most of the Social Democratic leaders, although his attitude toward their leadership was hardly enthusiastic.

One of his early contacts with a socialist party was a lecture he gave in 1919 to a group of Independent Social Democrats in Berlin-Zehlendorf, an event that prompted the Brandenburg church consistory to call on him to account for his political activities.[9] Here as elsewhere Tillich spoke from within the orbit of

9. *See* "Answer to an Inquiry of the Protestant Consistory at Brandenburg," trans. Mrs. Douglas Stange, *Metanoia* (Cambridge, Massachusetts), vol. 3, no. 3 (September 1971).

"Social Democracy." He was not a supporter of Bolshevism, which, due to the success of the October Revolution of 1917 in Russia, became an important political option in Germany, especially in the early and in the last years of Weimar. Tillich was opposed to the Russian-influenced Communists; he was also critical of the Social Democrats, as is evident in *The Socialist Decision*. He considered the Social Democratic party (SPD) rigid in theory, excessively calculating in method, and unimaginative and halfhearted in politics. From the beginning, Tillich stood on the critical left wing of democratic socialism, searching for a third way beyond Marxism-Leninism and mere reformism.

The most important influence on Tillich's developing religious socialism came from the small circle of intellectuals who gathered around him and Mennicke in Berlin during the hectic first five years of the Weimar Republic. In this informal circle, which met every other week in a participant's home for intense discussion, Tillich learned the ins and outs of socialist theory and practice, debated the challenge of Karl Barth's dialectical theology, and deepened and clarified his own "theology of politics." Repulsed by the vulgar Marxism of current socialism, the members of the "Kairos Circle" shared the conviction that a rethinking of socialist fundamentals was required. This emphasis on theory, as well as the lay, secular, and nonecclesiastical character of the circle, marked it off from other groups of religious socialists. Tillich said that he "considered himself thoroughly an evangelical-Lutheran Christian" who knew how all his ideas were conditioned by that standpoint, yet he insisted that the group be open to others besides Christians.[10] Many of the dozen members of the diverse circle had no attachment to the church but were drawn to the circle out of concern for the ethical and spiritual basis of socialism.

According to Eduard Heimann, Tillich was the "head" of the circle and Mennicke, who edited its little periodical, *Blätter für*

10. *Blätter für religiösen Sozialismus*, vol. 1, no. 1 (Easter 1920), p. 2 (Tillich's remarks as reported by Karl Mennicke).

religiösen Sozialismus (1920–1927), was its "heart."[11] Adolf
Lowe, then a civil servant, and Heimann, son of a leading Social
Democratic politician and already a recognized socialist econo-
mist, provided the "substructure" for Tillich's religious socialism.
The sociologist Alexander Rüstow, a free thinker and atheist, was
Tillich's rival. "His discussions with Tillich were doubtless the
highpoint of our meetings," Heimann has remarked.[12] Another
regular was Arnold Wolfers, a Swiss lawyer who was director of
the new *Deutsche Hochschule für Politik* (German Academy of
Politics). (The present volume began as a lecture at the
Hochschule in October 1931). In the give and take of this company Tillich's religious socialism matured.

The biweekly conversations of the Kairos Circle ended in 1924
when Tillich and others left Berlin for new academic positions.
Tillich, however, maintained his working alliance with Mennicke,
Lowe, and Heimann and continued to identify his religious socialism by reference to them. By the middle of the decade a
semblance of stability was present in the republic and Tillich
articulated a new sense of realism, a "believing realism," in contrast to what he now saw as his earlier unrealistic enthusiasm.
More and more cut off from the church, Tillich moved deeper
into the socialist milieu, pursuing further his searching reevalua-
tion of socialist theory from the theological point of view.
Through articles, books, and lectures his ideas gained a wider
hearing. He discovered some new allies among young socialists,
particularly the "Hofgeismar Circle," a group of proletarian youth
who challenged the orthodoxy of the SPD, especially on the questions of state and nation. It is they to whom Tillich refers in the
present treatise as "the younger generation of socialists."

On Pentecost weekend in 1928, Tillich along with Heimann,
Lowe, and Mennicke joined nearly eighty other religious social-

11. "Brief von Prof. Dr. Eduard Heimann an den Verfasser über die
einzelnen Mitglieder des Kairos-Kreises," Appendix 1 in Eberhard Amelung,
Die Gestalt der Liebe (Gütersloh: Gerd Mohn, 1972), p. 215.
12. Ibid., p. 216. Cf. also, for a general discussion by Heimann of Tillich's
thought in this period, his essay "Tillich's Doctrine of Religious Socialism" in
Kegley and Bretall, eds., *The Theology of Paul Tillich*, pp. 312–325.

ists, young socialists and others for a three-day conference at Heppenheim-on-the-Bergstrasse (near Heidelberg) to discuss "the weakening of confidence in the life-forming power of socialist ideas in our time."[13] United in their distress over the stagnant condition of the SPD, the participants were, however, split over the meaning of a renewed socialism. Hendrik de Man, whose writings had made him the center of controversy in German socialism, called for a non-Marxist "ethical socialism." In response, Heimann rejected an approach based only on moral appeal and argued for a dialectical socialism. This of course was also the position of Tillich. In the ensuing discussion he supported Heimann. "We stand before the decision: Do we see the coming of the *Gestalt* that is developing in the proletariat or don't we? The socialist is one who thinks that the existing tension expressed in the proletarian situation proclaims the new, developing *Gestalt*. This is dialectical thinking."[14]

For Tillich, dialectic and its proper understanding was the crucial element in socialist theory. Tillich believed that de Man's popular, nondialectical thinking as well as the party's mechanical interpretation of the dialectic were both inadequate. His discussion of "expectation" in *The Socialist Decision* is his most elaborate attempt to lay out the true meaning of historical dialectics, the theoretical foundation of socialism.

The spirit of Heppenheim achieved expression in the *Neue Blätter für den Sozialismus*, an independent socialist periodical that bore the subtitle "Journal for Spiritual and Political Formation." Tillich was the key person in initiating this publication and, as an editor, in shaping its direction. He persuaded the reluctant August Rathmann, a young socialist from the Hofgeismar Circle, to be managing editor. Convinced that he could not influence the socialist movement from outside the political party, Tillich joined the SPD in spite of his strong disagreement with its reformist

---

13. *Sozialismus aus dem Glauben* (Zürich: Rotaphel-Verlag, 1929), p. 243. This book records the discussion of the Heppenheim meeting. Others who participated included Martin Buber, Leonhard Ragaz, Hugo Sinzheimer, August Rathmann, Mennicke and Lowe.

14. Ibid., p. 103.

policies. He also proposed that in order to avoid misunderstanding (from both the "religious" and "socialist" sides), the designation "religious" be omitted from the title. In January 1930, the first issue of the *Neue Blätter* appeared with Tillich contributing the lead article, "Socialism."[15] The magazine was published monthly, reaching a circulation of 3,000, until June 1933 when, after repeated confiscations, the Nazis forbade its publication.

Besides regular meetings with his coworkers around the *Neue Blätter*, Tillich also took part in a more politically reserved, theoretically oriented discussion group in Frankfurt in the early 1930s. When in the Foreword to the present work he acknowledges this Frankfurt circle, he is referring to the conversation he carried on with his friends at the University, including members of the Institute of Social Research. Shortly after he had become professor of philosophy in 1929, Tillich had been instrumental in creating a new chair of "social philosophy" for Max Horkheimer, a position that allowed Horkheimer to become Director of the Institute. Tillich, Horkheimer, other members of what would become the famous "Frankfurt School"—Theodore Adorno, Leo Lowenthal, and Friedrich Pollock—and other faculty such as Karl Mannheim, Kurt Reizler, Lowe, and Mennicke, met together for what Tillich called his "Frankfurt Conversation." Tillich, though more closely related to the SPD than was the Frankfurt School, shared with the proponents of critical theory the intention to return to the Hegelian sources of the Marxist dialectic and to reconstruct socialist theory on this basis.[16]

Efforts to revitalize Marxist philosophy received an unexpected boost in 1932 when J. P. Mayer and Siegfried Landshut, two

15. *GW*, 2, pp. 139–150. *See* August Rathmann's "Tillich als religiöser Sozialist" in *GW*, 13 for a discussion of Tillich's role in the founding of the *Neue Blätter*, esp. pp. 566–7.

16. Martin Jay in his *The Dialectical Imagination* (Boston: Little, Brown and Company, 1973) refers to the friendship the members of the Frankfurt School had with Tillich. The memorial volume *Werk und Wirken Paul Tillichs: Ein Gedenkbuch* (Stuttgart: Evangelisches Verlagswerk, 1967) contains comments on Tillich by Horkheimer and Adorno. Tillich's relationship to the Frankfurt School and their critical theory then and later is a subject that deserves further research.

contributors to the *Neue Blätter*, discovered and published Marx's hitherto unknown writings, the *Economic and Philosophical Manuscripts of 1844*. These works of the young Marx confirmed Tillich's earlier insight that Marx was much more dependent on Hegel and much less the dogmatic materialist and narrow empiricist that so many of his followers had made him to be. Already in *The Socialist Decision* he appeals to the young Marx to support his own theoretical concerns. These fragments become an important source for Tillich's interpretation of Marx as a "secular prophet" and an "existentialist." Yet Tillich does not dismiss the older Marx, insisting, even in 1932, that the "real" Marx is a unity of the two, i.e., "Marx in the context of his development" (cf. below, Foreword, note 4). The present work is important, among other reasons, for its analysis and critique of Marxist theory (see especially part 3, chapter 2).

It was Tillich's special contribution to place the whole discussion of socialism within a theological perspective. In this volume the theological element is more implicit than explicit, yet it is clearly there. In offering a theological interpretation of socialism and other political realities, Tillich is utilizing some of the basic concepts that he was developing during these same years in other dimensions of his thought, for example, his broadened concept of "religion." "The decisive idea of religious socialism," he had written, "is that religion does not have to do with a specific religious sphere but with God's dealing with the world, and that therefore, it is possible that God's activity may be more clearly seen in a profane, even anti-Christian, phenomenon like socialism than in the explicitly religious sphere of the church."[17] Such a view opens the way for a theological understanding of an apparently secular movement like socialism.

Tillich sees socialism, the self-expression of the proletariat, as

17. "Religious Socialism," in Paul Tillich, *Political Expectation* (New York: Harper & Row, 1971), p. 44. *See also* the Introduction to this volume for comments on Tillich's religious socialism by the editor of the volume, James Luther Adams.

For a thorough exposition of Tillich's understanding of religion, *see* his three essays collected in the volume *What is Religion?*, also ed. and intro. James Luther Adams (New York: Harper, 1969).

having given meaning to the proletariat in a meaningless world, a meaning that is ultimately religious, for it transcends the empirical and points to that which is "finally meant," to the Unconditional. Tillich was convinced that no one really understands socialism if he or she overlooks its religious dimension. But this can be overlooked, because it is hidden in nonreligious, rational forms. Thus Tillich interprets socialism as "prophetism on the soil of an autonomous, self-sufficient world" (cf. below, p. 101). His goal is to make conscious the faith working in socialism, and on this basis to transform it.

In other times, argued Tillich, this same faith had been expressed with the prophetic-eschatological symbol of the "kingdom of God." His theological interpretation turns on this symbol. One might even say that the theological thrust of his religious socialism was to discover the concrete social and political meaning of the prayer, "Thy kingdom come." The kingdom comes in history, yet remains transcendent; the kingdom is "at hand," but it cannot be possessed. Its character is paradoxical: the transcendent is not in an undialectical opposition to history, but shows its genuine transcendence by breaking into history, shattering and changing it. From the side of the human subject, the proper response is one of expectation, an attitude that looks toward the future as something promised and something demanded, as a gift and a task. Tillich relates this understanding directly to socialism:

In the struggle *against* a demonized society and *for* a meaningful society, religious socialism discerns a necessary expression for the expectation of the kingdom of God. . . . It regards this unity of the socialist dialectic, a unity of expectation and demand of that which is to come, as a conceptual unity and at the same time as a concrete and contemporary transformation of the Christian eschatological tension.[18]

Here in *The Socialist Decision* as nowhere else, Tillich draws upon this eschatological strand of his thought and brings it to bear on the political situation. The "prophetic" perspective, which

18. Ibid., p. 50.

he summarizes with the future-oriented symbol of expectation, gives unity and depth to the book. Tillich's elaborate discussion of expectation in many ways foreshadows the theological preoccupation with "hope" several decades later. This perspective, as he explains, has its historical source in the Jewish prophets, its anthropological roots in human existence itself, and its political significance in the socialist movement. It expresses the meaning of the "socialist principle," on the basis of which Tillich offers a subtle, internal critique of socialist theory and practice and a bold appeal to rebuild the movement.

Interestingly, Tillich structures his book on the basis of an anthropological consideration. In contrast to some other socialist intellectuals (Horkheimer, for example), Tillich sees positive value in the new interest in the question of the nature of human existence sparked by Martin Heidegger and Max Scheler. The questions that Paul Gauguin once wrote on a canvas—"From where do we come? Who are we? Where are we going?"—are ones that for Tillich are perennially significant for political theory. The question of "Whence?"—answered by "myths of origin"—is the foundation for all conservative and romantic political thinking. The question of "Whither?" or "For what end?"—the eschatological question—means the "breaking" of the myths of origin and is the root of liberal, democratic, and socialist thinking. For Tillich this second root takes precedence over the first: "the powers of origin" are subordinated to (but not eliminated by) justice. This means, for example, that the values connected with the past, such as regional, cultural, and ethnic heritages, may and should be acknowledged, but the demand of the future has priority.

Tillich's political analysis and evaluation is built on this interpretation of the "two roots" of human existence. From this starting point, Tillich offers a discerning appraisal of German society on the eve of the Nazi takeover. He presents a penetrating discussion and refutation of what he calls the "two forms of political romanticism," the conservative form represented by the Prussian landowners, the old military leaders, the Evangelical churches, and other groups in power before the November Revolution of 1919, and the revolutionary form represented by Adolf Hitler and the middle-income groups supporting National Socialism. Both of these adhered uncritically to the myths of origin, rejecting the demand of justice. Likewise he critically examines the presuppositions of capitalist society as expressed in the "bourgeois principle," which views reality as a set of objects that can be rationally controlled. In so doing, Tillich charges, it reduces persons to things and cuts them off from the creative origins of life. Bourgeois society, he further asserts, rests on a belief in "automatic harmony"—a belief that is contradicted by the reality of the class struggle. It is the dominance of this bourgeois principle among socialists themselves, Tillich contends, that is responsible for the dilemma in which socialism finds itself, a dilemma which he seeks to address with a new formulation of the "socialist principle" that draws upon its religious roots.

Tillich explores these diverse phenomena in their social, political, economic, cultural, religious, and philosophical facets. In a fashion characteristic of Tillich, *The Socialist Decision* gives conceptual order to an immense range of human experience from a consciously developed, all-embracing perspective. And he writes this book not as a detached observer, but as one summoning his readers to decision.

The year 1932, during which the present work was written, was an ominous time marked by growing chaos and pending collapse. Depression and massive unemployment had thrown the fragile Weimar Republic into disarray. Political leadership had fallen into antirepublican, antidemocratic, antisocialist hands. On 20 July 1932, the new, reactionary Chancellor Franz von Papen (a striking example of the conservative form of political romanticism) illegally took control of the Prussian government, the last stronghold of the Social Democrats; the socialists offered no resistance. The indecisive, reformist SDP battled the dogmatic, revolutionary Communists for the loyalty of the workers while the militant, right-wing National Socialists (a parody on the concept of socialism) made impressive gains among the middle class. Tillich foresaw that the future might well be one of "barbarism." Already he recognized the possibility of war. If the militaristic, nationalistic right were victorious, insisted Tillich, "a self-annihilating struggle of the European peoples is inevitable" (cf. below, p. 161). He believed, however, that socialism, a renewed and transformed socialism, still offered a possibility for averting this future. Germany faced a choice, and the choice was clear: either barbarism or genuine socialism. Tillich was appealing for "the socialist decision," but Germany was "deciding" for Nazism.

Tillich wrote the bulk of *The Socialist Decision* during the summer of 1932 in the mountains of Sils Maria, Switzerland, where he was vacationing with his wife Hannah and his friends Adolf Grimme, Mannheim, and Lowe.[19] Grimme, a religious socialist, had been the Prussian Minister of Education from 1930 to 1932. The sociologist Mannheim and the economist Lowe were Tillich's colleagues at Frankfurt. In the morning, Tillich would go into the woods and write, and in the afternoon he and Lowe would discuss what he had written, a circumstance that accounts for his expression of special gratitude to Lowe in the Foreword. Apparently he completed the writing at the home of some friends in Potsdam.[20] Tillich signed the Foreword on November 9 (on the fourteenth and last anniversary of the proclamation of the "German Republic"), and he issued his announcement of the book in the December issue of the *Neue Blätter*. It was published early in 1933, appearing as part of the series *Die sozialistische Aktion*, sponsored by the *Neue Blätter*.

But it was too late. Historical events foreclosed any genuine socialist decision; on 30 January 1933, Adolf Hitler took power, and the barbaric future began. *The Socialist Decision* was suppressed and all the socialist literature of Alfred Protte, Tillich's publisher, was confiscated. Later, the remaining copies of the work were destroyed when the Protte warehouse in Potsdam was

19. The following is based on the interview with Adolf Lowe on 4 May 1972. *See also* Hannah Tillich, *From Time to Time* (New York: Stein and Day, 1973), p. 147.

20. Mrs. Lily Pincus, a German émigré psychotherapist living in London, in a letter to Prof. James L. Adams on 2 February 1972, wrote: "About *Die sozialistische Entscheidung:* I think you know that much of it was written in our house in Potsdam, and I remember Paulus passing up and down the garden in writing-pains."

leveled by Allied bombs. The book's public existence thus was extremely short-lived, and no reviews of it were printed. Like other anti-Nazi material, *The Socialist Decision* was consumed by the fires of repression.

Although the book never achieved its deserved recognition, it was important for Tillich and his friends. On 13 April 1933, Tillich's name appeared on the first list of intellectuals to be "purged," and along with Mannheim, Lowe, Horkheimer, Hermann Heller, Hugo Sinzheimer, and others, he was dismissed from his teaching position. The immediate cause of the dismissal was Tillich's defense of some students attacked by Nazi "Brown Shirts" and his insistence that the latter be punished. Jobless, yet eager to remain in Germany in order to influence the political situation, Tillich traveled throughout the country to confer with his friends as to what he might do. He wanted to write for the underground press, but his friends told him that his style was too easily recognizable, and that he therefore would be a greater liability than a help! In the fall, as it was becoming increasingly clear that he would have to go into exile, he visited a high official of the Nazi Ministry of Education, who had requested to see him. During their conversation, the official is reported to have asked Tillich to revoke *The Socialist Decision* in exchange for a prestigious chair in theology at the University of Berlin. Tillich's reply was to laugh in his face.[21] Soon thereafter he left for the United States.

This episode took on the significance of a prophetic encounter for Tillich's socialist friends, and *The Socialist Decision* became for them a symbol of courage and resistance. During the next dozen years of terror and war, the few surviving copies of the book were quietly passed from hand to hand among these people, "contributing to their resolve to resist the Hitler absurdity."[22] No

21. This final incident was related by Dr. Lowe in the aforementioned interview. *See also* Hannah Tillich's description of their last months in Germany, *From Time to Time*, pp. 147–156.

22. August Rathmann, "Einleitung," in his edition of *Die sozialistische Entscheidung*, p. 7. Rathmann brought out this second edition of *The Socialist Decision* in 1948, but it received little notice in the postwar setting, a

other book by Tillich was so fully enmeshed in and finally over-
whelmed by the events of his day, and yet none of his books so
clearly and forcefully spoke to the historical and structural crisis
confronting his society. Perhaps this explains in part Tillich's later
remark to James Luther Adams that of all his books, he was most
proud of *The Socialist Decision*. And because of its timely "prophetic word" as well as its stress on the attitude of expectation,
many readers will also agree with Adolf Lowe that this writing is
Tillich's "most prophetic book" as well as his "most Jewish
book."[23]

This book has been translated into English for the first time
after a lapse of more than forty years. The historical distance
between that time and now is considerable. Yet this book can
perhaps be studied with greater appreciation and profit today
than at any other time since it was first published. The primary
reason for this is that the relation between the socialist and Christian traditions is more fluid today than at any time since the
1930s.

The euphoria of the early Christian-Marxist dialogue of the
1960s is gone; nevertheless, this dialogue opened up long-closed
doors separating the two. Marxist intellectuals such as Ernst
Bloch, Milan Machovec, Leszek Kolakowski, Vitezslav Gardav-
sky, Roger Garaudy, Horkheimer, and Adorno have demonstrated the continuing vitality of the Marxist tradition by raising
self-critical questions and by reevaluating the traditional Marxist
attitude toward religion. Garaudy has gone so far as to speak of a
"Christian Marxism." On the Christian side, a good many thinkers
in both Europe and America have come to doubt that a truly
human society is possible within the structures of capitalism, and

---

time that Tillich considered a "void." In his Introduction, Rathmann lists
Theodor Haubach, Carl Mierendorff, and Adolf Reichwein as members of
the *Neue Blätter* circle who were killed for their participation in the preparation of the plot to kill Hitler on 20 July 1944.

23. From the interview with Lowe, 24 May 1972. *See further*, for the
placement of this book within the total context of Tillich's life and work, the
biography by Wilhelm and Marion Pauck, *Paul Tillich: His Life and
Thought* (vol. 1, "Life," New York: Harper & Row, 1976; vol. 2, forth-
coming).

have become more and more critical of the church's endorsement of bourgeois life; they are beginning to make their own "socialist decisions." In the oppressive conditions of Latin America, theologians of liberation are seeking new ways of integrating faith and critical social thought in their own situations, and a movement called "Christiars for Socialism" has emerged. Thus in the elusive search for economic and political justice and for a meaningful society, the relation of Marxism and Christianity is once again an open question. The Paul Tillich of *The Socialist Decision* would have felt at home in this world. Readers of the work may find their own possibilities and limitations illumined by his similar struggles in his own time and space.

Translator's Note

The German original of this book, *Die sozialistische Entschei-dung*, was first published in 1933 (Potsdam: Alfred Protte) and was reprinted in 1948 (Offenbach am Main: Bollwerk). The translation has been made from the text as printed in Tillich's *Gesammelte Werke*, vol. 2 (Stuttgart: Evangelisches Verlagswerk, 1962), corrected where necessary by reference to the 1933 edition. The footnotes are given as they originally appeared in 1933, rather than being updated as was done for the *Gesammelte Werke*; thus the reader can be aware of the editions actually used by the author at the time of writing. Supplementary data provided by the undersigned, including references to existing English transla-tions of the works cited, have been enclosed in square brackets. In addition to this amplification of Tillich's footnotes, translator's notes of an explanatory nature have been provided at a number of places in the main text.

The rendering of certain terms presented special problems. Til-lich makes much of the distinction between *Sein* and *Bewusstsein* ("being" and "consciousness"), which constitutes a play on words that is impossible to convey in English, unless one were to render it "being" and "being conscious." The term *Sein*, as is well known, carries special overtones for Tillich; for this reason, I have translated it consistently as "being," even though a phrase such as *menschliches Sein* ("human being") could in many places have been rendered more idiomatically as "human existence" or "human life."

A complicating factor is that in an effort to be faithful to the inclusive nature of the German term *Mensch* (plural, *Menschen*) and to avoid possible male-only connotations in English, most occurrences of this term have been translated as "person," "human being," "humanity," or "humankind" rather than man, men, or mankind. Hence the reader must be alert to the distinction between *a* human being (*Mensch*), human beings (*Menschen*), and human being (*menschliches Sein*) in the generic and ontological sense. For similar reasons, a phrase such as *sozialistische Menschenauffassung* has been rendered "socialist view of human nature" rather than "socialist doctrine of man."

Verdinglichung, literally "thingification," has been rendered as "objectification." Alternatives would have been "reification" or, more graphically, "dehumanization." It is recognized that this may not correspond precisely with English versions of works by other authors with a comparable intellectual background, such as Martin Heidegger or Herbert Marcuse, but it seems most adequate in the present context.

Only a small portion of the present work, namely, the Introduction, has appeared in English before. This was published under the title "The Two Roots of Political Thinking" in the collection of Tillich's essays entitled *The Interpretation of History*, translated by N. A. Rasetzki and Elsa L. Talmey (New York: Scribner's, 1936). This section has been retranslated for the present volume.

I should like to thank those who have been of material assistance in the making of this translation, especially Professor Roy J. Enquist, who contributed a major portion of the initial draft; also Professors Carl E. Braaten and Wilhelm C. Linss, A. Jean Lesher, Dennis P. McCann, and Erich W. Geldbach, who provided further invaluable assistance at various points in the process; and Professor James Luther Adams, who originally recruited me for the project and who has provided continual advice and encouragement during the period of its execution. The translation has been in many ways a collaborative enterprise; however, final responsibility for its defects must be assumed by the undersigned.

Franklin Sherman
Lutheran School of Theology at Chicago

Foreword

The socialist decision is a decision *of* socialism and a decision *for* socialism. What follows is a summons to this twofold decision. We shall establish the grounds for this decision, describe its nature, and demonstrate its necessity. The socialist decision is required of two groups: of those who are the bearers of socialism today, and of those who today are its opponents, but who in the future will also have to be its bearers. The demand for a socialist decision is addressed to both these groups: to the first, in the sense of a new decision for socialism—a new vision of its nature, its problems, its difficulties, and its coming form. That a new decision of socialists for socialism is needed, is shown clearly by its present fate. We shall unveil the causes of this fate and explore the possibilities of averting it.

But a socialist decision is demanded also of the enemies of socialism. Above all, those groups that today carry the word *socialism* in their names* must be brought to a real socialist decision. We shall show why by their present attitude they not only negate socialism but also threaten the future of the nation and of Western civilization. These groups are not to become a part of

* This included the Nazis, the full name of whose party was *National-sozialistische Deutsche Arbeiterpartei* (National Socialist German Workers' Party).—TRANS.

the proletariat but rather are to be drawn to its side, so that by a common socialist decision the fate of death now facing the peoples of Europe can be averted. Only the socialist decision can avert this fate. It is for this reason that we are summoned to it.

Socialism, to be sure, is not written off as dead today in the same sense as liberalism is. There would be much less justification for doing so. At the present time, however, powerful spiritual and political forces, especially in Germany, are turning against a particular form of socialism, falsely called "Marxism" out of ignorance and propagandistic motives. The social grounds for this struggle are manifest, and particularly with regard to National Socialism have long since been clearly and impressively demonstrated.[1] This having been said, however, nothing has yet been decided concerning the rightness or wrongness of this struggle against socialism. The struggle could be directed rightly against particular forms of socialism, but wrongly against the socialist principle. This is precisely the assumption from which this book proceeds. It aims to show what socialism and Marxism really are. It therefore assumes that the picture socialism presents to its opponents is not the necessary form of socialism, nor is it the true expression of the socialist principle appropriate to the present social situation.

This enterprise is not possible, however, without an attempt to envision and to grasp anew the socialist principle as the sustaining power of socialism. This book therefore involves not only a struggle *for* socialism; it involves also, and even more, a struggle *about* socialism. It strives for a new understanding of what socialism can be and must be today. Such endeavors are sharply opposed by a dogmatically bound socialism that is tied to certain thought patterns, indeed to a limited number of slogans, and which lacks the ability even to entertain any ideas or to listen to any suggestions that run counter to these fixed lines. Against such an attitude there are no spiritual weapons; it can only be shattered through the course of events themselves. Certainly it has nothing to do with scientific socialism, although it loves to use this name. For the prime requisite of the scientific attitude is ever and again to question one's own presuppositions, to take the ideas of others as seriously as one's own and not to dismiss them out of hand.[2]

The political events of recent years have been decisive in providing the impulse to begin and complete this book: the decline of the political influence of the Social Democrats, the apparently final split in the proletarian working class, the triumphal advance of National Socialism, the consolidation of the late-capitalistic powers on a military basis, the increasingly perilous situation in foreign affairs. These factors make it imperative that socialism reflect on itself in a fundamental way, above all on its implicit assumptions. For the implicit basis on which socialism lives has a greater influence on its development and on the image it presents than what it explicitly says and does. Our intention is to make explicit what is implicit, not just in order to display it, but in order to test its appropriateness in the light of the principle of socialism and of the present social situation. A movement that no longer questions the rightness of its own assumptions has become ossified. No matter how seriously embattled it might be, this does not justify the refusal to undertake such questioning. For the opponents' weapons are forged from the rigidity of the socialist movement, not from its self-criticism. Take from them the possibility of their forging and sharpening such weapons, and every assault can be withstood.

Three generations are presently contending with one another in socialist circles. There is an older generation that even today forms the intellectual and political leadership of the Social Democratic party. This generation is rooted in the period of militant and progressive socialism, and its worldview is determined by the positivism of the late nineteenth century. Its ideology culminates in a "scientific" faith in a process of development that will lead inevitably to a socialist society. According to this view, the socialist struggle is itself a calculable consequence of this calculable process. The socialist struggle does not create the process but is created by it; step by step, economic development makes victory unavoidable. Even the setbacks, large and small, are seen in terms of this necessity and prove nothing against the final victory.

On the other hand there is a younger generation that experienced the Russian Revolution and witnessed the tremendous power of will at work in it, which against all expectations proved victorious in that economically most backward country. At the same time it saw how in the mature capitalistic states, feudal and bourgeois powers entrenched themselves anew, opening the way to a feudal capitalism. This generation has thereby been led toward a voluntaristic, ethical socialism that at the same time better satisfied its impulse for "socialist action" (a concept stemming from the younger circle of the *Neue Blätter*).* Simultaneously, such tendencies were strengthened by developments in Western socialism, especially the writings of Hendrik de Man.[3]

In between these is the generation whose experience and thinking forms the background of this book. It holds fast to Marxism and defends it against the activism of the younger generation; but it rejects the form in which the older generation took it over from the nineteenth century. It goes back to the real Marx[4] and to a concept of dialectic in which necessity and freedom are conjoined. Thereby it gains a perspective on the bourgeois elements that nineteenth-century socialism took over, contrary to its own nature. And it is free to appreciate the prebourgeois forces that have never disappeared among the bourgeoisie, regarding which socialism has yet to establish its own position. The burden of our generation is to be a bridge. It is the good fortune of our generation that it *can* still be a bridge, not only between the generations but also between the groups that must be the bearers of socialism.

This presentation stays as far away as possible from the tactical questions involved in the opposition between Social Democracy and Communism. Its aim is to deal with fundamental issues, and it takes the view that this opposition lies less at the level of fundamentals than at the level of the practical, the sociological, and the temperamental. A successful clarification and transformation of the fundamental issues would do much to soften the sharp opposition among the socialist parties. For the moment, to be

---

* The *Neue Blätter für den Sozialismus. See* below, note 6.—TRANS.

sure, little is to be expected, since the dogmatic rigidity of Communism makes the intrusion of new ideas and impulses almost impossible. The fate of German socialism will therefore, also in the future, be decided in the Social Democratic party (insofar as parties as such can be decisive).[5]

This presentation does not deal, either, with the problems posed by the Soviet Union. The reason is that the intention here is to tackle the socialist problem in the context of German socialism. The developments in Russia are of course of the greatest interest for any treatment of socialism—but not in the sense of a model whose solutions can be adopted. Russia is experiencing simultaneously both socialism and the triumph of the rational principle. Russian socialism directly followed Russian absolutism. This is decisive for judging both the revolution itself and the subsequent course of events down to the present time. At one point, incidentally, Russian socialism corresponds entirely to a basic postulate of the present work: in Russia, the proletariat and the peasantry carried through the revolution together, the agricultural question remaining till today the most important problem of domestic policy for the Soviets. But in this respect too, as in every other, German socialism must seek its own solutions. Socialism cannot wait for its realization until the proletarian world revolution. It must succeed nationally, even though this is possible only within limits. The actual realization of socialism in any given nation means more for world socialism than all the utopian talk about world revolution.

The present volume grew out of a lecture given at the Hochschule für Politik [Academy of Politics] in October, 1931. The process of working out the lecture brought so much new material to the fore and required the working through of so many pressing ideas that a book resulted. This does not mean, however, that the movement of ideas which finds preliminary expression here has been concluded. It must proceed further, beyond this book, perhaps even in contradiction to it. But precisely to make this possible, a line had to be drawn. For this there were also political and personal reasons.

The ideas originate from many years of preoccupation with the problems of socialism, and especially from the joint labors of friends and working groups in Berlin and Frankfurt. I should like to mention particularly only Eduard Heimann, to whom this book is dedicated, and Adolf Lowe, for whose help I am most deeply indebted.

While my earlier writings originated in connection with the *Blätter für religiösen Sozialismus*, my more recent ones, particularly this one, appear in connection with the *Neue Blätter für den Sozialismus*. By avoiding the name "religious socialism," which has been challenged (with good reason) from the religious as well as the socialist side, and which moreover has given rise to constant confusion, it is possible to express more clearly our actual position.[6] That the religious roots of these ideas have by no means been severed is shown by the concepts chosen to play a central role as well as by the sections dealing with socialist belief and with socialism's attitude toward culture and religion. But the religious element now remains more than before the subsoil from which the ideas arise, rather than the content of the ideas themselves. This corresponds entirely to our situation vis-à-vis religion. It is what at one time was being called for under the name of "believing realism."[*]

From this position it was of course impossible to compete with the kind of apocalypticism espoused by the "Tatkreis"[**] and groups connected with it, and which has met with such astonishing literary success—not even to mention the National Socialist writings. Socialism has no right to intoxicate people with visions of the future and then dash their hopes. It has to be sober in its analysis, and sober in the attitude of expectation it assumes. It must unmask all ideologies, including its own. Only with apprehension and with the sharpest of self-criticism may it seek for syntheses. The harshness of the proletarian fate and the burden

---

[*] Cf. Tillich, *The Religious Situation*, trans. H. Richard Niebuhr (New York: Holt and Company, 1932), where, however, the phrase (*gläubiger Realismus*) is rendered "belief-ful realism." The German original of this book, *Die religiöse Lage der Gegenwart*, dates from 1925.—TRANS.

[**] A group associated with the neoconservative journal *Die Tat*, edited by Eugen Diederichs until his death in 1927 and from 1928 to 1933 by Hans Zehrer.—TRANS.

of the socialist struggle against the "powers that be" allow us no ecstasies or glorifications. Socialism requires the clearest, most sober realism, but this must be a believing realism, a realism of expectation. The following comments are to be understood from this point of view. They may seem ecstatic to unbelieving realists, while striking faith-filled idealists as dull and laborious, but this does not speak against their truth. The path of socialism is laborious in every step; but it leads to victory if it takes this labor upon itself in clear-sighted yet venturesome expectation.

Introduction: The Two Roots
of Political Thought[1]

1. Human Being and Political Consciousness

It is not always necessary to inquire into the roots of a spiritual or social phenomenon. When sturdy growth shows us that the roots are unimpaired, such an inquiry is superfluous. But if the plant begins to become bent and twisted, if growth ceases and life begins to fade away, then it is essential to ask: What is the condition of the roots? This is the situation of socialism, particularly of its strongest branch, German socialism. The political events of recent months have found it in a gravely weakened state.[2] And this situation is caused not only by the events of recent years. The causes go back much farther, back to the second half of the nineteenth century, and partly even to the historical situation at the time of socialism's origin. The most urgent task in these coming years of self-examination is to seek the causes of this weakening. This can only be accomplished by answering the question of roots.

However, as soon as we ask the question regarding the roots of socialist thought, it becomes necessary to go further. For socialism is a countermovement, in a double sense: it is directly a countermovement against bourgeois society, and indirectly—together with bourgeois society—a countermovement against feudal-patriarchal forms of society. Therefore in order to understand socialism in terms of its roots, it is necessary to uncover also the roots of the political thinking opposed to it.

1

The roots of political thought must be sought in human being itself. Without some notion of human nature, of its powers and tensions, one cannot make any statements about the foundations of political existence and thought. Without a doctrine of human nature, there can be no theory of political tendencies that is more than a depiction of their external form. A doctrine of human nature, however, cannot be worked out here. It must be presupposed, and at best it can create for itself a favorable hearing by its capacity to illuminate political thought.[3]

Human beings differ from nature in that they are creatures with an internal duality. No matter where nature ends and humanity begins, no matter whether there are gradual transitions or a sudden leap between them, somewhere the difference becomes visible. Nature is a unified life-process, unfolding itself without question or demand, and bound by what it finds in itself and its environment. Humanity is a life-process that questions itself and its environment, placing demands on itself and its environment, which therefore is not one with itself. Rather, it has these two aspects: to exist in itself and simultaneously to stand over against itself, thinking about itself and knowing about itself. Human beings possess self-consciousness, or to contrast this with nature, they are beings who are internally dualized by virtue of their self-consciousness. Nature lacks this duality. We are not implying in these statements that human beings are composed of two independent parts, for example, of nature and spirit, or body and soul; rather, there is *one* being but twofold in its unity.

Even these very general definitions have consequences for any investigation of political thought. They make it impossible to derive political thinking from purely mental processes, from religious and moral demands or ideological judgments. Political thinking proceeds from human nature as a whole. It is rooted simultaneously in being and in consciousness, more precisely in the indissoluble unity of the two. *Therefore it is impossible to understand a system of political thought without uncovering the human and social reality in which it is rooted,* that is, the interrelation of drives and interests, of pressures and aspirations, which make up social reality. But it is equally impossible even to conceive of this reality as separate from consciousness, that is, to view consciousness and along with it political thought as mere by-products of being. *Every element of human and social being, down to the most primitive emotional drive, is shaped by consciousness.* Any effort to dissolve this connection ignores the first and most important characteristic of human nature, and therefore results in distortions in the total picture of that nature.

To point out that there is a consciousness that does not correspond to being, the so-called "false consciousness," proves nothing against the unity of being and consciousness.[4] For the very concept of a "false consciousness" is only possible and such a thing is only knowable if there is a true consciousness. A true consciousness, however, is one that arises out of being and at the same time determines it. It is not one without the other. For human nature is a unity in its duality, and the two roots of all political thinking grow out of this unity.

Human beings find themselves in existence; they find themselves as they find their environment, and as this latter finds them and itself. But to find oneself means that one does not originate from oneself; it means to have an origin that is not oneself, or—in the pregnant phrase of Martin Heidegger—to be "thrown" into the world. The human question concerning the "Whence" of existence arises out of this situation. Only later does it appear as a philosophical question. But it has always been a question; and its first and permanently normative answer is enshrined in myth.

The origin is creative. Something new springs into being, something that did not previously exist and now is something with its own character over against the origin. We experience ourselves as posited, yet also as independent. Our life proceeds in a tension between dependence on the origin and independence. For the origin does not let us go; it is not something that was and is no longer, once we become independent selves. Rather, we are continually dependent on the origin; it bears us, it creates us anew at every moment, and thereby holds us fast. The origin brings us forth as something new and singular; but it takes us, as such, back to the origin again. Just in being born we become involved in having to die. "It is necessary that things should pass away into

that from which they are born," declares the first saying handed
down to us in Western philosophy.* Our life runs its course in
terms of birth, development and death. No living thing can transcend the limits set by its birth; development is the growing and
passing away of what comes from the origin and returns to it.
This has been expressed in myth in infinitely diverse ways, according to the things and events in which a particular group
envisages its origin. In all mythology, however, there resounds
the cyclical law of birth and death. Every myth is a myth of
origin, that is, an answer to the question about the "Whence" of
existence and an expression of dependence on the origin and on
its power. *The consciousness oriented to the myth of origin is the
root of all conservative and romantic thought in politics.*

But human beings not only find themselves in existence; they
not only know themselves to be posited and withdrawn in the
cycle of birth and death, like all living things. They experience a
demand that frees them from being simply bound to what is
given, and which compels them to add to the question "Whence?"
[*Woher*] the question "Whither?" [*Wozu*]. With this question
the cycle is broken in principle and humankind is elevated beyond the sphere of merely living things. For the demand calls for
something that does not yet exist but should exist, should come to
fulfillment. A being that experiences a demand is no longer
simply bound to the origin. Human life involves more than a
mere development of what already is. Through the demand, humanity is directed to what ought to be. And what ought to be
does not emerge with the unfolding of what is; if it did, it would
be something that is, rather than something that ought to be. This
means, however, that the demand that confronts humanity is an
unconditional demand. The question "Whither?" is not contained
within the limits of the question "Whence?" It is something unconditionally new that transcends what is new and what is old
within the sphere of mere development. Through human beings,
something unconditionally new is to be realized; this is the mean-

---

* Fragment of Anaximander, as rendered in Werner Jaeger, *Paideia: The
Ideals of Greek Culture*, trans. Gilbert Highet (New York: Oxford University
Press, 1945), vol. 1, p. 159.—TRANS.

ing of the demand that they experience, and which they are able
to experience because in them being is twofold. For the human
person is not only an individual, a self, but also has knowledge
about himself or herself, and thereby the possibility of transcending what is found within the self and around the self. This is
human freedom, not that one has a so-called "free will," but that
as a human being one is not bound to what one finds in existence,
that one is subject to a demand that something unconditionally
new should be realized through oneself. Thus the cycle of birth
and death is broken; the existence and the actions of human
beings are not confined within a mere development of their
origin. Wherever this consciousness prevails, the tie to the origin
has been dissolved in principle and the myth of origin has been
broken in principle. *The breaking of the myth of origin by the
unconditional demand is the root of liberal, democratic, and socialist thought in politics.*

Yet we cannot stop with a simple opposition between these two
aspects of human existence. The demand that human beings experience is unconditional, but it is not alien to human nature. If it
were alien to our nature, it would be of no concern to us and we
could not perceive it as a demand upon us. It affects us only
because it places before us, in the form of a demand, our own
essence. Therein alone is grounded the unconditionality and inescapability with which the demand confronts us and must be
affirmed by us. But if the demand is our own essence, it is
grounded in our origin. The questions "Whence?" and "Whither?"
do not belong to two different worlds. And yet, the demand is
something unconditionally new over against the origin. This indicates that *the origin is ambiguous.* There is a split in it between
the true and the actual origin. *The actual origin is not the origin
in truth.* It is not the fulfillment of what is intended for humanity
from the origin. The fulfillment of the origin lies rather in what
confronts us as a demand, as an ought. The "Whence" of humanity finds its fulfillment in the "Whither." The actual origin is
contradicted by the true origin, not absolutely and in every respect, for the actual origin—in order to be actual at all—must
participate in the true origin; it expresses it, but at the same time

both obscures it and distorts it. The mentality oriented solely to the myth of origin knows nothing of this ambiguity of the origin. Therefore it clings to the origin and feels that it is a sacrilege to go beyond it.[5] The ambiguity of the origin is first revealed to it when the experience of the unconditional demand frees this consciousness from bondage to the origin.

The demand is directed towards the fulfillment of the true origin. Now a person experiences an unconditional demand only from another person. The demand becomes concrete in the "I-Thou" encounter. The content of the demand is therefore that the "thou" be accorded the same dignity as the "I"; this is the dignity of being free, of being the bearer of the fulfillment implied in the origin. This recognition of the equal dignity of the "Thou" and the "I" is justice.[6] *The demand that separates from the ambiguous origin is the demand of justice.* From the unbroken origin proceed powers that are in tension with one another; they seek dominion and destroy each other. From the unbroken origin there comes the power of being, the rising and perishing of forces that "pay one another the penalty and compensation for their injustice according to the ordinance of time," as is asserted in the already quoted first statement of Greek philosophy.* The unconditional demand transcends this tragic cycle of existence. It confronts the power and impotence of being with justice, arising from the demand. And yet, the contrast is not absolute, for the ought is the fulfillment of the is. *Justice is the true power of being.* In it the intention of the origin is fulfilled.

The result is that the two elements of human being and the two roots of political thought are related in such a way that the demand is superior to mere origin and justice is superior to the mere power of being. The question "Whither?" is of higher rank than the question "Whence?" *Only when the myth of origin is broken and its ambiguity disclosed may it enter into political thinking.*

---

* Cf. above, p. 4.—TRANS.

2. *Approach and Standpoint*

The relationship between the two roots of political thought is not one of simple juxtaposition. The demand is superior to the origin. Therefore, a consideration of political trends cannot proceed on the assumption that they are typically human attitudes of equal justification. *The concept of the typical is not applicable where decisions are required.* But this is the case when an unconditioned demand is made. One cannot do it justice by a comparative or typological approach; already by using such an approach one has avoided the demand and in fact has conceded that the alternative is justified, by placing it on the same level with the demand in an allegedly neutral description. At bottom this holds true of every attempt to understand spiritual things. One cannot be a spectator of the spirit; it makes demands, it calls for decisions. No one can understand socialism who has not experienced its demand for justice as a demand made on oneself. *Whoever has not struggled with the spirit of socialism can speak about it only from the outside, which is to say, in fact not at all.*

It is otherwise in the case of political trends in which the bond of origin is predominant. They also must be understood; in them, too, spirit speaks to spirit and requires a decision. But here the decision is to lead precisely in the direction of renouncing inquiry and decision and reverting to mere being. In affirming the origin, one seeks by its help to avoid what is demanded. To be sure, one uses the mind, but against the mind; one inquires, but against the spirit of inquiry; one demands, but against the demand. One seeks by spiritual means to draw the spirit back into the bondage of being. This is the inner contradiction of political romanticism in all its forms. For this reason it is basically impossible to decide for it intellectually. As long as the bond of origin remains unbroken, no decision can be made, because no choice exists. But once it is broken, a decision in its favor can only mean the suspension of all free decision. No attempt to establish a spiritual basis for political romanticism can escape this contradiction.

The roots of political thought do not lie in ideas but in human being, that is, in being that is twofold, conscious being. This means that political thinking is necessarily an expression of political being, of a social situation. Thought itself cannot be understood without taking into account the social realities out of which political thought arises. The roots of political thinking cannot be equally effective in every period and every group. The predominance of one side or the other is dependent on a particular social situation, on particular groups and forms of authority. It is further dependent on particular social-psychological structures which interact with the objective social situation. By means of their social-psychological effects (by which they in turn are influenced), the economic and governmental forms of a given period tend to make certain elements of human being predominate at that time.

This interconnection between social being and political consciousness gives rise to a question that must be answered before we can undertake the discussion of political problems, and especially the problems of socialism. Socialism, as will be demonstrated, is the direct expression of the proletarian situation. How then is it possible, one could ask, to criticize socialism or to argue for it from a position that is not itself proletarian? The answer is that consciousness is indeed dependent on being, but they are interconnected in a functional, not a biographical way. Certain ideas, whether they were set forth by aristocrats or bourgeoisie, had the function of expressing bourgeois being. And certain ideas, whether set forth by bourgeoisie or proletarians, have the function of expressing proletarian being. The fact that it was primarily aristocrats who prepared the way for bourgeois society, and the bourgeois who gave to the proletariat its self-consciousness, shows how little depends on the biographical relationship. Indeed, the distance between being and consciousness can become the very condition for the raising of being to consciousness. *Knowledge entails not only relationship to being but also distance from it.* Therefore the person whose confidence in his or her own group and class situation has been deeply shaken is in the best position to provide an alien class with its self-consciousness. The best examples of this are Marx and Lenin. They serve at the very outset to lift the correlation of social situation and political thought from the biographical to the functional sphere.[8]

3. Principle and Reality

The word *principle* is used to refer to the summarizing characterization of a political group. The following considerations have been decisive in the choice of this term. It is the task of thinking to select from a variety of phenomena that which makes them belong together and which makes the individual intelligible from the standpoint of the whole. This task is usually accomplished by means of a concept of the "essence" of a thing. Since Plato, epistemology in the West has been dominated by the problem of the relation between essence and appearance. But now it has been shown that the logic of essence is inadequate in face of historical realities.[9] The "essence of a historical phenomenon" is an empty abstraction from which the living power of history has been expelled. Nevertheless, we cannot dispense with summarizing characterizations when we are dealing with a coherent movement. It is not enough to refer to historical continuity, since some selection must be made out of the infinite abundance of continuously linked events. Therefore we must seek another method of historical characterization. In place of the concept of essence, which is derived from the knowledge of nature, we must introduce a dynamic concept, in accordance with the character of history. *A concept is dynamic if it contains the possibility of making understandable new and unexpected realizations of a historical origin.* I should like to call such concepts "principles." A principle does not contain the abstract universality of a mass of individual phenomena; it contains the real possibility, the *dynamis*, the power of a historical reality. The principle can never be abstracted from the multiplicity of its individual realizations, for it always stands in a critical and judging relation to its reality, and not only in a foundational and supporting relation. There can be no contradiction between essence and appearance, but there can be a contradiction between principle and realization. It is possible to have access to a principle, therefore, only through an act of understanding that always contains at the same time an element of decision. No one understands, for example, the Protestant principle on the basis of everything that has ever happened in and to Protestantism. It can be understood only on the basis of a decision, from the standpoint of which the whole history of Protestantism is not only grasped but also criticized. This consideration is bound up with the other consideration, that spirit can be understood only by a spiritual decision. Thus socialism also is to be understood only in terms of a socialist principle that is gained only by a socialist decision, and which is the standpoint both for interpreting and for judging socialist reality.

Principle must not be confused with idea or with universal concept or the like. A principle is the real power that supports a historical phenomenon, giving it the possibility to actualize itself anew and yet in continuity with the past. The principle of political romanticism is the inner power of the groups bearing political romanticism, expressed in concepts and understood in terms of the roots of human and historical being. The principle of socialism is not a socialist idea; it is the proletarian situation interpreted in terms of its dynamics. "Principle," therefore, is not an ideological concept, but one that is descriptive of reality. *A principle is the power of a historical reality, grasped in concepts.*[10]

PART ONE:

POLITICAL ROMANTICISM,

ITS PRINCIPLE

AND ITS CONTRADICTION

CHAPTER 1

The Presuppositions of Political Romanticism

1. Mythical Powers of Origin

The myth of origin envisions the beginning of humankind in elemental, superhuman figures of various kinds. Common to them all is the fact that they are expressions of the human tie to father and mother, and that by the power of this tie they want to hold consciousness fast, not allowing it to escape from their dominion. Myth research, depth psychology, sociology, and ontology have worked together in a unique way to unveil this primordial human situation.[1]

In the mythical consciousness, the origin is never viewed abstractly as origin, but always concretely in terms of *specific powers of origin*. Just as human existence itself is differentiated, so are its origins, as well as the powers of origin which are envisioned in myth and represented in cult. It is possible, however, to bring together some of the universally prevalent types of powers of origin, those which also have a markedly political significance.

The most widespread and at the same time the most concrete power of origin is *the soil*. The vegetative layer of human existence and of all existence is grounded in it. It generates life from itself, supports and nourishes it, and then takes it back into itself again. It holds everything under the spell of the cycle of birth and death. The deities of the soil are the holiest; they are the last to let the consciousness go free. If a person has lost contact with the soil that produced him, that person has lost his god and its supporting power, and is miserable, homeless, impotent. Here is the root of the feeling for the soil of farmers and landowners as well as the feeling for home of people in country towns, and in a final extension, of the national feeling for soil and home.

The sense of dependence on the origin is expressed in two ways, as confinement to the cycle of vegetative existence and its eternally constant laws, and at the same time as dependence upon superior powers that in incalculable ways bestow good and evil, and before which one must bow. The cultic posture culminates in the elevating of one's own power of being through the divine power of being in transport and ecstasy, but at the same time in a readiness to surrender one's own power of being, in death, for the sake of the divine. All of these elements of bondage to the soil have continuing effects in the most advanced cultures and repeatedly break loose from aesthetic and political forms of rationalization in a violent manner (frenzy, will to power, self-destruction).

The animal form of origin—*the origin of blood*—develops out of the vegetative form represented by the soil. This is a narrower and more definite power of origin. Animal power proves itself in encounter with other animal powers in a process of selection through struggle and breeding. The origin differentiates itself into a noble and a common type. Concepts such as "noble blood," "noble race," "noble lineage" appear. Noble origin is divine origin, in the sense of special election. The closer one is to the origin, the greater one's power of being and the more noble one is. Power of being in the animal sense is not brute strength, but rather a fullness of life that has been given form. These two things—closeness to the origin and a high level of formation—do not contradict each other, but belong together. For to be given form is to attain to being. Therefore the unity of youth and form is the highest symbol of animal power.

The enhancement of being stemming from animal power is expressed in heroic ecstasy in which life and death, courage and melancholy, are one. "Noble" means being consecrated to death, the return to the origin; not, however, out of mere resignation or obedience to duty, but ecstatically. Social dominance, the ruling power of the noble race, follows directly from this power of being which proves itself in its readiness to die.[2]

In addition to the origin of soil and blood there is the origin coming from the *social group*. None of these three excludes the others. Yet each one involves a particular aspect that predominates and that can provoke conflicts. This is particularly the case with social origin. It is most clearly manifest where people have detached themselves from the soil and where, as with nomads, the social group becomes the immediate sustainer of individuals. The unity of the tribe is seen in the ancestor; the blood relationship becomes a relationship of partriarchal rule. While the origin of soil and blood is more commonly expressed in the mother symbol, in the social sphere the father symbol predominates. The father combines supportive and demanding aspects, whereas in the mother, in soil and blood, the immediate law of origin is more visible. The tie to the father therefore takes the form of a tie to the primordial demand, to the primeval ordinance that passes as a heritage from the father to the son. The line of ancestors is an expression both of blood origin and of the continuity of the social group and its ordinances. Ecstasy here takes the form of being imbued with the power of the group's origin, and of the assertion and implementation of an age-old heritage over against all novelty, of tradition over against progress. Frequently this entails a rejection of the ecstasies of fertility and heroism, because these threaten the demand of the father as socially established and defined. This primeval law shapes the unconscious; it works through the line of ancestors, holding the individual in thrall within the circle of the group and its patriarchal rule. And yet it is the demanding character of the father-origin that makes it at all possible to break the myth of origin. It is still only a possibility, however; the origin still rules. Integration into the group still is demanded. Liberation from the origin becomes real only when a break with the social group also can be demanded, i.e., in prophetism.

In each of these three types of myth of origin, that which comes into existence is viewed and determined from the standpoint of the origin. This orientation of consciousness to the origin is maintained and made explicit by the *priesthood*. It interprets the origin as primordial revelation. Thus the power of origin, which is immediately effective and formative in the other configurations of life, here becomes the object of special acts, both in the realm of myth and in the realm of behavior. The priesthood preserves the sacred tradition; it preserves and presents anew the connection with the powers of origin. It stands in an enduring special relation to the "Whence" of human being. Ecstasy, considered as a pure infusion of the transcendent powers of origin, is fostered, and that which is revealed is guarded as mystery. The vital ecstasies are formed, limited, and transformed, without, however, being negated. The explicit character of the shaping power of the origin leads to explicitness and awareness in general; the power of the word is experienced as a magical, but also partly as a rational, power. Yet the limits of the original revelation are not transgressed in principle.

Corresponding further to the explicitness of the shaping power of religion is its tendency to assume a particular social form. To the extent that the priesthood detaches itself from the concrete powers of origin and directs itself to the origin as such, it acquires sociological independence as the bearer of religion, i.e. (in agreement with the meaning of the word), of the tie to the origin. Since, however, the abstract must derive its content and richness from the concrete, the priesthood is always at the same time the consecrating and the confirming agency for the other powers and their formation, and these in turn are dependent on such priestly confirmation.[3]

The origin embodies the law of *cyclical motion*: whatever proceeds from it must return to it. Wherever the origin is in control, nothing new can happen. If the "Whence" predominates it is impossible to take the "Whither" seriously. The cycle can be made wider or narrower, but it remains a cycle. It is narrowest in the vegetative sphere—blossoming, bearing fruit, and decaying. It is wider in the animal sphere, where history unfolds in the encounter of powers, in struggle, in the rising and passing away of power relations. The cycle is still wider in the social sphere, where in the relation of the individual to the group, law and morality are formed and transformed and the question "Whither?" makes its appearance. But this question is not raised so long as the domination of the father is unchallenged. The priestly mysteries and revelations are related to the "Whence," and their cults and initiations are oriented to the return to origin.[4]

This means, however, that here time is always under the *domination of space*. Time has not achieved its true nature, its real power, when it is viewed in cyclical or circular terms. For the power of time lies in its irreversible forward motion towards the new, towards the "Whither."[5] As long as it does not have this meaning, it is merely a modification of space. For all groups bound to the origin, therefore, existence is defined in terms of maintaining and creating space. For them to lose their space is to lose their existence. This is equally true of the bondage to the soil of vegetative existence and its sociological analogue, the peasant class, and of the mastery of the soil in the animal sphere, which to be sure is less dependent on a single plot of ground, but still remains limited, in its foraging or fighting, to the area under its control. Among the animals, the individual is assigned and held to a space or status [*Stand*] in accordance, above all, with its prowess in battle. This applies also to the social group that sustains the individual by guaranteeing each person a share in the social space or sphere of existence and by requiring each in turn to be integrated into this sphere and its structures. Thus space for family and nation arises in connection with the space of soil and domination. Originally, even the priesthood was space-bound, consecrating the given sphere of soil, power, and social life in its particularity, i.e., imparting to it the transcendent power of origin. The spatially bound cycle of existence with its traditional forms and laws and the given relationships of soil and dominance receive their consecration from the origin. The standard of criticism is the original state, even where the life-process forces into existence something actually new. The new can only be accepted in the name of the original.

Ontologically speaking, this means: *being is holy.* For being is the origin of everything that exists, and being constitutes the criterion of everything that exists: the power of being is the highest standard. Being is itself the truth and the norm. It determines both the form and the limits of its space. Ontology is rooted in the myth of origin; it is bound to space. It must even make time into something spatial. Ontology is the final and most abstract version of the myth of origin.[6]

2. The Break with the Myth of Origin in Judaism

The myth of origin necessarily takes a *polytheistic* form. The basic structure of space as coexistence side by side drives all spatially bound existence into polytheistic mythology. Not the origin in general, but the concrete origin is holy; for it is this that sustains, that gives power and being. Where the origin has become general and abstract, the myth of origin has receded into the background. Where the latter predominates, it consecrates a particular space—this soil, this lineage, this social group, this nation. But alongside this there are other soils, other lineages, other nations; they receive their consecration from *their* god and *their* priesthood. But this does not stop with a simple coexistence. The creative powers of origin press beyond the original point of emergence. They want to subject to themselves other powers of origin and to enlarge their space. They make a universal claim; their ultimate goal is to encompass all of space. This is based on the origin itself, in two respects. The pure origin, the sheer power of being, the unbroken drive toward realization, is inherently without limits. In nature, limits are predetermined by the origin; every being has its particular domain. Human beings, however, possess the possibility of going beyond every limited domain. Their possibility is their temptation, the temptation to want to enlarge their limited space to limitless space. This striving is justified in principle by the transcendent grounding of the power of origin by the priesthood. To be bound to a finite, conditioned space, however, contradicts the essence of the transcendent, the unconditional. One's own god is addressed as the Almighty, as the "ruler of heaven and earth." The limited origin is transformed into an unlimited one, without ceasing to be limited. And one's particular god becomes god of the whole world, without ceasing to be a particular god. But the contradiction goes further: the mythical consciousness creates all-embracing unities and tries to overcome polytheism by the *imperialism of one god*, that is, of *one* space. The result is the unification of many lands in one cultic union and the merging of lineages, tribes, and nations under one sovereign rule. It also results (most often subsequently) in a priestly fusion of myths and, finally, in philosophical abstraction —i.e., in the idea of the totality of all that is, the logical imperialism of which is an appropriate expression of the mythical-political imperialism with which it is connected.

The original attachment to the soil, however, is stronger than the power of the all-embracing unity. Out of a particular soil with its creatively originating character, forces of particularization continually break forth, tearing apart the sovereign unities. Polarization and demonic divisiveness have the last word on soil that is space-bound.

Domination by space is broken where a tendency in this direction has been established—in the social group, and in connection with the demand implied by the father symbol. *Being loses its immediacy through the "ought."* The question of the "ought" cannot be answered by reference to what is. "The good transcends being" (Plato).

There can be no "ought" on the basis of unbroken being and sacred space. Unbroken being does not have an imperative character. To be sure, there are good and bad forms of being; there are ecstatically heightened forms of experience and normal ones; but as forms of *being*, they are all equal to each other. What "is" does not, by virtue of its mere "isness," exhibit any differentiation. On the basis of mere being, there is no other norm than being. However, the norm of mere being is power of being and its opposite, powerlessness. This means, practically, that might makes right. This is the only possible ethic on the basis of a consistent myth of origin. But of course, this is no ethic, but a mere assertion, and an unfounded use of two names—might and right—to refer to the same thing.[7] Thinking that is bound to the categories of space already surpasses itself (mostly without knowing it) whenever it applies ethical norms.

It is the significance of *Jewish prophetism* to have fought explicitly against the myth of origin and the attachment to space and to have conquered them. On the basis of a powerful social myth of origin, Jewish prophetism radicalized the social imperative to the point of freeing itself from the bond of origin. God is free from the soil, the sacred land, not because he has conquered foreign lands, but precisely because he has led foreign conquerors into his own land in order to punish the "people of his inheritance" and to subject them to an unconditional demand. The bond of origin between God and his people is broken if the bond of the law is broken by the people. Thus the myth of origin is shattered —and this is the world-historical mission of Jewish prophetism. With the breaking of the tie to the soil, the other forms of the myth of origin also lose their power. The sacred aristocracy, including the monarchy, is rejected for the sake of righteousness. The claim of belonging to the people avails nothing in face of the unconditional demand, on account of which the alien can be held in equal, indeed, in higher esteem. The priestly tradition is not abolished but is judged by the demand of righteousness, and its cultic aspects are devalued. The breaking of the myth of origin becomes evident, finally, in the prophets' opposition to the priests.[8]

Positively this means that the independent character of time is recognized; it means the *elevation of time above space*. Time acquires a direction; it moves towards something that did not exist but will exist and, once it is attained, will not be lost again. The expectation of a "new heaven and a new earth" signifies the expectation of a reality that is not subject to the structure of being, that cannot be grasped ontologically. The old and the new being cannot be subsumed under the same concept of being. The new being is intrinsically unontological. It cannot be derived from the original state. It goes beyond the origin into a second phase, so to speak, the phase of *the new in history*. Thereby the origin itself appears in altered guise. It receives the character of a beginning. In the myth of origin there is no temporal beginning; existent things forever emanate from the origin and return to it. Being is not the beginning of existing things, but rather their

constant root. Prophetism transforms the origin into the beginning of the historical process: the creation, which itself is pictured
symbolically as an historical act. Corresponding to the beginning,
there is a goal and a "center," i.e., the event that gives the process
its meaning and direction.[9] In this way the beside-each-otherness
of space loses its significance in face of the unity of temporal
directionality. Polytheism is broken by the monotheism of the
God who effects his will in history and of the community that
serves as the bearer of history. Thus Judaism could become a
"people without space" without perishing. It became a "people of
time," overcoming the beside-each-otherness and against-each-
otherness of the several spaces.[10]

Christianity, through severe struggles, made the spirit of Judaism its own foundation. It took over the Old Testament, the idea
of creation, and the historical concepts and defended them
against attempts to reinterpret the Christian event according to
the myth of origin. In these struggles Christianity came to the
very edge of extinction as an independent religion. At last, however, it won out and affirmed the Old Testament as its indispensable basis.

Yet the myth of origin left its mark on Christianity in two
respects: first, in the development of a Christian priesthood,
which adopted countless elements from polytheism and the myth
of origin and transformed the primitive Christian "tension towards what lies ahead" into devotion to the given, to the sacred
tradition. And secondly, by the entrance of Christianity into the
world of nations and their various forms of life related to the
myth of origin. Thus the powers of soil, blood, group, and status,
which had been broken by prophetism, reappeared. The power of
being as such was declared holy in the name of Christianity. This
comes to clearest expression when the Christian church serves to
confirm the given sociopolitical power structures and the nation's
claims to dominance.

Over against this it remains the *function of the Jewish spirit* to
raise the prophetic protest, both in Judaism and in Christianity,
against every new attempt to revive such bondage to the myth of
origin, and to help time, the unconditional demand, and the

"Whither" to be victorious over space, mere being, and the "Whence." The spirit of Judaism is therefore the necessary and eternal enemy of political romanticism. Anti-Semitism is an essential element in political romanticism. Christianity, however, by virtue of its principle, belongs radically and unambiguously on the side of Judaism in this conflict. Any wavering on this issue is apostasy from itself, involving compromise and denial of the shattering—manifest in the cross—of all holiness of being, even the highest religious being. A Christianity that abandons its prophetic foundation by allying itself with political romanticism has lost its own identity.[11]

Of course, prophetism and Judaism cannot simply be equated. Old Testament prophetism is the persistent struggle of the "spirit of Judaism" with the *realities of Jewish national life*. For the actual life of the Jewish nation, like the actual life of every nation, is by nature pagan. Hence, we see the foolishness of certain nationalistic demands that the Old Testament be dismissed as an expression of an alien nationality. In fact, the Old Testament writings are a continuous testimony to the struggle of prophetic Judaism against pagan, national Judaism. For this reason, and solely for this reason, the Old Testament is a book for humanity— because in it the particular, the bondage to space and blood and nationalism, are seen as things to be fought against.

Now it is the tragedy of Judaism that its historical fate not only broke the hegemony of the powers of origin, but also frequently dissolved them altogether, insofar as no new ties to the soil were created in their place (though this did come to pass in east-European Judaism). This negative element, the critical dissolution of the myth of origin instead of its prophetic transformation, gives to anti-Semitism and political romanticism an apparent justification for resisting this tendency. But this justification is invalid, because such resistance, instead of strengthening the prophetic element in Judaism against the dissolving tendency, fights against the prophetic element itself and thereby weakens its power, even within Judaism. The "Jewish problem" can only be solved by a decisive affirmation of the prophetic attack on the dominion of the myth of origin and all thinking bound to space. Only in this way can the pagan element in the Christian peoples and the negatively critical element in Judaism simultaneously be overcome. A *secessio judaica*,* on the other hand, would mean a relapse into the barbarism and demonry of an existence totally bound to space.

3. The Break with the Myth of Origin in the Enlightenment and the Romantic Reaction

Bondage to the origin and expectation of the end have something in common: they both transcend that which is given in space and time. For this reason, expectation of the end does not simply cancel the bond of origin; it breaks its authority and changes its character, but does not abrogate it. The father, understood as origin, remains also for the prophetic consciousness as bearer of the demand, as ruler of history, and as creator of the new. It is not prophetism but the autonomous consciousness that first breaks away from every kind of tie to the father.[12]

The *autonomous consciousness* suppresses the dimension of the origin, the depth dimension of existence, so to speak. Finite forms in their finitude become the objects of knowledge and manipulation. Also the goal of such manipulation remains in the realm of finitude; it can always be stretched out further, indeed indefinitely, but it does not break through the limits of finitude. Such expectation directs itself to progress, not to the really "new."

The *suppression of the dimension of origin* occurs in relation to all the powers of origin. The soil becomes a means for the production of goods, which indeed is "given," but is to be dealt with technically. The incalculable elements that arise out of the general context af nature are gradually repressed. The insecurity that remains is rendered harmless by equalizing different spaces through new technologies of transportation. The particular soil is no longer binding, since an overarching spatial unity has been created by technical means. Technical space, which in principle is identical with terrestrial space as such, overcomes beside-each-

---

* Jewish secession or withdrawal.—Trans.

otherness and against-each-otherness. The potency of animal existence disappears before the power of rational efficiency. Rational
education for all, that favorite weapon of the Enlightenment,
breaks through the status structure and its ties. Reason, common
to all, takes the place of the divine election of the nobility. Traditions cannot withstand the demands for a rational structuring of
existence. Revelation becomes a historical process as "the education of the human race." The priesthood is deprived of its power
through the rational criticism of miracles and mysteries. Ecstasies
are supplanted by sober research and purposeful action. Entities
are not viewed as impenetrable, primordial phenomena that
coinhere with one another, but as a lawful sequence of analyzable
elements. Just as there is nothing that cannot be solved by thinking, so there is nothing that cannot be shaped by action. The
myth of origin has lost its power.

Prophetism and *autonomy* have in common the fact that for
both, the myth of origin has been shattered. Therefore, it is not
entirely meaningless to consider the spirit of prophetism—or to
put it anti-Semitically: Judaism—to be partly responsible for the
Enlightenment. With respect to the Enlightenment in Germany,
this also has a certain historical justification. But the fact of the
Greek Enlightenment, the fact of Renaissance humanism, and the
fact of the opposition between Protestantism and humanism show
that prophetism and autonomy proceed from different and independent sources. Expressed in terms of the history of religions,
prophetism retains its connection with the father, whereas autonomy has forsaken this connection. The attempt to unite the two
was first made in Liberal Protestantism. This attempt is of decisive significance because as a result it has become evident that
prophetism as well as autonomy in their isolation from each other
eventually fall back again into the myth of origin. Prophetism
settles down into a new priesthood that makes the prophetic
proclamation into a binding priestly rule. And autonomy for its
part falls into an emptiness whose negative character is the best
breeding-ground for a new outbreak of positive paganism.

The powers of the myth of origin, to be sure, have been broken
by the Enlightenment; their symbols and forms of expression

have been destroyed; but they have not been eradicated as powers, neither as psychological nor as social powers.

Viewed from the perspective of the psyche, there are three powers that resist the rationality of the Enlightenment: *eros, fate,* and *death.* There is eros, that wants to be in union with the primal power of existence prior to any analysis, and which is set in opposition, especially by youth, to the ways in which we rationally order the world. There is fate, that manifests itself as the primordial power resisting all efforts to shape or calculate existence, especially in times of crises for the autonomous spiritual and social situation. And there is death, that as the limit of the finite inevitably poses the question of the meaning of finitude, thus leading beyond finitude.

Viewed in societal perspective, there are the *ancient powers—* the nobility, the landowners, the peasantry, the artisans, the priesthood—which, although broken and largely subjected to the technical world order, still are not abolished; they react with instinctive self-defense against being incorporated into the rational system, whether directly or in their new role as officers, bureaucrats, and employees. Of course, they finally do accommodate themselves to the rational system on account of its material power and its economic advantages. In the moment, however, that this material power is reduced and the advantages turn into disadvantages, the instinctive counterforces are revived with double strength. In addition, there are the outlying areas of other countries and regions that have not yet been so thoroughly affected by rationalism. There is also the essentially maternal psychological structure of the woman, which is just as opposed to the prophetic demand of the father as to the autonomous protest against both father and mother. Then there are young people, who on the one hand retain the old ties with the origin, and on the other hand, contribute new powers of origin of a revolutionary kind. Out of the convergence of all these forces, political romanticism arises. It is an attempt to restore the broken myth of origin, both spiritually and socially.

Political romanticism is, thus, the countermovement to prophetism and the Enlightenment on the basis of a spiritual and social

*situation that is determined by prophetism and the Enlighten-
ment.* It is thereby compelled to fight under presuppositions that
it denies and with methods that it attacks in its opponents. It is
forced to use the ethical categories of prophetism and to portray
itself as a higher ethos (for example, as a higher justice), even
though the myth of origin as such excludes ethics. And it is forced
to use rational analysis as a means of establishing itself (for example, historical, sociological, and psychological investigations),
and thus to appeal to the very thing it distrusts in principle as
alien to the origin. In this way the theories of political romanticism arise; despite the frequently brilliant way in which they are
developed, they cannot escape the contradiction of having to
establish the irrational by rational means. In this way, too, there
emerges the praxis of political romanticism, which on the soil of
a consciously organized society has to adopt the very rational
forms of organization it seeks to abolish. The myth of origin can
only return—unbroken, as is necessary for it—if the society in
which it has been broken comes to an end. The Middle Ages were
only possible because antiquity and its whole system of rational
perception and shaping of the world had come to an end. And
there will be a new Middle Ages only if Western society has to
atone for its Enlightenment with the end of its own possibility of
life. Only in the case of certain extreme ideas does political romanticism venture to draw this conclusion and affirm the coming
of a Western form of the *fellaheen* society.* If, however, it
shrinks from this, it lands in the contradiction between the necessity of using rational forms and at the same time fighting against
them. It cannot escape this contradiction, and for this very reason
it is romanticism.

---

* Cf. below, chap. 2, note 22.—Trans.

CHAPTER 2

The Forms of Political Romanticism

1. Conservative and Revolutionary Forms

Political romanticism can assume either of two forms: it can be *conservative* or *revolutionary*.[13] These two forms can be combined in many ways, but they can also stand in opposition to one another. The conservative form is based on the attempt to defend the spiritual and social residues of the bond of origin against the autonomous system, and whenever possible to restore past forms. It appears in groups that have not yet been completely integrated into bourgeois society: primarily landowners, peasants, nobles, priests, artisans. The revolutionary form tries to gain a basis for new ties to the origin by a devastating attack on the rational system. It is carried out by those groups that have entered into the inner structure of the rational system, without having lost continuity with the groups of origin from which they are descended. But now they feel threatened by complete absorption into the system, on the one hand, and by the mechanization and loss of status which this system effects, on the other hand. Here we find primarily office employees, certain groups of bureaucrats, and those intellectuals who have no chance of being incorporated into the rational system; but there are also some farmers and artisans who are being hit specially hard by the crisis, to the point of hopelessness. These two groups can become partners in common action, but at the same time they have inner tensions, tensions that become sharper as it becomes clearer that the revolutionary groups want to get rid not only of the drawbacks of the rational system but also of the advantages it has given to the conservative groups.

In addition to the difference between the conservative and revolutionary forms of political romanticism, and partly overlapping it, there is the difference between its *transcendent* and *naturalistic* forms. The first type preserves the myth of origin in its traditional religious form and on this basis tries to define a worldview and a structure of society. Behind it stand the churches, insofar as they have linked themselves to political romanticism, as well as the old conservative groups influenced by the church. The second type interprets the myth of origin in terms of a philosophy of life, thus depriving it of its essentially mythical character, even when it speaks of a new myth. Here we find primarily the groups of a revolutionary character. However, conservative groups that have become thoroughly integrated into bourgeois society also tend to argue their demands in this-worldly and naturalistic terms.[14]

Thus it is quite clear that this opposition, too, is not an exclusive one. The reason for this is found in the historical situation, for even the transcendent tendency is unable to avoid the power of the Enlightenment and its critique of myth. The naturalistic tendency, on the other hand, if it is to take seriously its own idea of myth, must go beyond the natural-immanental approach. Practically, however, this difference is of the greatest importance for the structuring of groups within political romanticism.

The basic concept of conservative romanticism is the concept of the *organic*, whereas revolutionary romanticism, with a better grasp of the contradiction between the idea of organism and rational political activity, uses concepts such as movement, action, *élan*, life-urge, etc. It thus represents the idea of the *dynamic* in the true sense.

The concept of the dynamic is indispensable for the delineation of a certain level of reality and a certain view of the world oriented to it. It should be used only in this sense and not—as often happens—be extended recklessly and thus emptied of meaning. Being should be called "dynamic" in so far as it is moving from possibility to reality; it is the not-yet-formed in which, however, there lies the possibility and the power of form.[15] The dynamic would then be a new category, distinct from the organic as well as from the mechanical, a category that would be appropriate to the social situation of revolutionary political romanticism. The idea of the dynamic can express at the same time both the will to break through the calculability and compulsion of the rational system, thus "melting down" its elements and making them fluid, and the will no longer to be subject to the old forms that have been ideologically glorified by the notion of organism. Origin in the sense of the dynamic idea would mean the innovative [*das Entspringen*]; origin in the sense of the organic idea would mean the original [*das Ursprüngliche*]. Revolutionary romanticism wants to let something new originate; conservative romanticism seeks to rediscover what is original.

Many phenomena in our spiritual and political life today can be understood from this perspective—for example, the structural relationship (to be discussed below) between revolutionary romanticism and revolutionary socialism; the dynamic character of modern nonromantic Gestalt theory; expressionism in art; but above all, the politically decisive fact that the transcendent aspects of political romanticism stand in great tension with its revolutionary thrust. The priesthood is oriented to the original; it acknowledges the innovative only within the limits of priestly control.

The difficulties of revolutionary romanticism stem from the fact that it is concerned only with the innovative and not with the original. For as a political movement it must set certain goals. Since, however, it cannot draw these goals either from the traditions of the past, as conservatism does, nor from a rational analysis of the present, as in socialism, its concepts of the goal are unsettled, obscure, contradictory, and impractical. The negative aspect is far stronger than the positive. The power of this movement lies almost entirely in its movement, not in the expectation of that to which it is supposed to lead.

2. Return to the Powers of Origin

The two forms of political romanticism, despite the differences in their concept of the goal, are united in their desire to return to the origin—not in a general way, but to the particular powers of origin from which prophetism and bourgeois society have broken away. All their political demands are basically to be understood in terms of this return to origin.

The *return to the soil* is politically operative in the demand to maintain or restore the class of large landowners as well as the peasantry, both of which groups are economically obsolete and can exist only at the expense of the national economy as a whole. For the sake of the myth of the soil and the stratum of society that bears it, the national space is supposed to be cut off and isolated from the world economy. The technical space of human-kind is to be broken up into autarkic groups, and the possibility of an all-embracing unity is to be sacrificed. The price of a decrease in the standard of living, brought about not because of any crisis but as a matter of principle, is to be paid largely by the population not bound to the soil. The effort to point out the impossibility of adequately supporting the masses of the people from home soil, and thus to point to the spatial unity of the world economy, as a rational argument, makes no impression on the mythically aroused consciousness, or else it is dismissed by referring to the decline of population (which is a matter of dispute).[16]

The *return to the animal sphere* naturally plays the chief role in revolutionary romanticism. Blood and race are its fighting words. By means of a racial theory (to which its proponents seek to give scientific form), the superior power of being of one's own race is affirmed, foreign races and nations are disparaged, and the political and economic claims of supremacy for one's own nation are ideologically justified.

This mythology of blood assumes its most passionate forms in anti-Semitism, for here economic opposition is coupled with the rejection of the prophetic element in Judaism, a view that has given all Germanic blood-mythology a bad conscience ever since Christianization set in.

In half-contradiction to the belief in a race of noble birth, this racial theory demands racial breeding of a very rational sort, thus proving that the superior race has in any case disappeared as a reality. Otherwise it would not be necessary for it to make itself an object of theory and technique.

The blood-oriented proximity to origin of the *female sex* is used by political romanticism to remove women from the public sector —spiritual, political, and economic—and put them back into the patriarchically structured family, to deprive them of their political rights and to cast back the relation between the sexes either into the old aristocratic pattern of male dominance or into the legalistic confines of the lower middle class. Of course, in line with the general contradictions within political romanticism, woman's power of rational judgment and her public activity are most emphatically enlisted for this purpose.

The *return to the social group* is expressed in the appeal for "community" which is so common to all forms of political romanticism. This appeal reflects an intense longing for a supporting group, in contrast to the spiritual, economic, and political autonomy of the individual in the rational system. It is the desire to be supported and made secure, a desire that increases all the more as the critical social situation makes the individual aware of his or her insecurity. Connected with this longing for security are powers of eros such as those that erupted especially in the youth movement, powers that seek to overcome the liberal competition of all against all in the economic struggle for existence. Likewise connected with this longing is the inner dissolution of the "son-religion," the desire to recover the ties to mother and father. Whereas the community as a whole is thereby vested with mother symbols—it is the embracing and supporting element that exists prior to the individual—the father is seen as the unity of the community and its head—as "monarch" in conservative and as "leader" [*Führer*] in revolutionary romanticism, and in both forms as the bearer and embodiment of the state. The longing for a charismatic leader is the naturalistic counterpart to the religious belief in monarchs elected and supported by the grace of God. In both forms, the return to the father myth of the social group is clear. The elevation of the state above society by political romanticism has the same motive. The state is the supporting and demanding father, in contrast to the society, in which every individual is on his own. But this does not apply to every state. The rational state that is democratically based and which guarantees a free social process is precisely the opposite of the state as father and origin. It is an abstract law that does not uphold the individual, but subjects the individual to an impersonal mechanism. Therefore, the call for a strong state is immediately changed into its opposite when the democratically based, rational state shows its power. It lacks the sacredness of a myth of origin. For the idea of a state founded on the myth of origin finds its fulfillment only in the sanctification of national soil and space, the animal power of being of one's own race, and the heroic readiness for sacrifice of the noble class. All this is epitomized in the myth of the authoritarian national state directed by a *Führer* or a monarch. This state exists for its own sake, and not for the sake of society or for all individuals. This notion of existing for itself, apart from the people who belong to it, certainly is a myth. It has reality only in the longing to return to the origin, the longing of masses who are hurting and exhausted in the freedom of the rational system.

But the contradiction of political romanticism shows itself here too. The call for community challenges the individual to create that which is supposed to precede the individual—the supporting group, the community, the state. It presents the demand, so to speak, for the son to create the mother and to call the father into being out of nothing. Hence political romanticism experiences its most severe disappointments just at this point; nowhere is the contradiction between longing and reality so painfully felt as here.[17]

3. *The Struggle concerning Traditions*

Between the origin and the present stands tradition. It is therefore of decisive importance in every respect for political romanticism to be able to relate itself to prebourgeois traditions.

The fact that there has been an almost two-hundred-year-old *break with traditions* in most sectors of life cannot, however, be wished away. Political romanticism, in the face of this, has only two possibilities: either to defend such islands of tradition as remain, even though they have become meaningless in the total structure of existence, or to attempt to revive the old, lost traditions. But a tradition that has been broken is really no longer a tradition, but a literary remembrance. The attempt to make tradition out of literary remembrances is the true mark of romanticism, on account of which it is called romanticism; and this is also the clearest expression of its inner contradiction.

Yet it must make this attempt if, while awaiting new traditions that will spring up in the future, it is not to face complete emptiness in the present. The latter is no longer possible for a political movement that has won some influence; it must seek traditions that it can place over against the present.

Traditions are as differentiated as the types of origin from which they stem. There are traditions of soil, place, region, and home; traditions of blood, family, clan, and nation; traditions of particular rank and calling; moral, legal, and religious traditions. In every case, tradition has two connotations: descent from an origin and subordination to the authority of the origin, i.e., of a special realm and its structure. Small as the practical value of these ideas may seem at the present time, their ideological power is strong, and thus their value as weapons against existing forms. Their attack is directed against universal humanistic education, against the leveling of moral standards and philosophies of life as a result of the uniform framework of social interchange; against the intellectual autonomy of the individual and the lack of inwardly authoritative criteria; against the openness of the professions to everyone and the lack of established social rankings; against the equalizing tendencies of the metropolis, in which many realms of life interpenetrate one another, and whose influences, through technical means such as radio and cinema, draw even the rural areas into this single unit. Finally, and chiefly, it is directed against the political autonomy of the individual, detached from all special traditions. Positively, the myth of tradition concentrates on the national tradition. It finds its climax in the demand to maintain this tradition, to strengthen it through the creation of a national historical legend, and to free it from international traditions. Political romanticism demands such a myth of tradition and sets about creating it.

To be sure, we see here again the inner contradiction of the return to the myth of origin. The creation of a *national tradition* must, in the context of life in the metropolis and its influence throughout the country, pass over all special traditions, the very traditions so important to the myth of origin. Nothing is more untraditional, in the national sense, than this struggle for a national tradition. What really has been handed down in Germany, and what has remained unbroken down to the present time, is the struggle of the various religious, political, and regional traditions with one another. A struggle of traditions, however, so long as it still has reality and has not been reduced to literature, can only be handed down by the protagonists, i.e., *not* as a unified national tradition. The attempt to create a unity bound to the origin by means of the old-Germanic heritage is completely hopeless, since as soon as the Germanic people appeared on the scene of history, they were grasped by the major streams of tradition already in existence and deprived of their original structure. To be sure, the Germanic substance was at work in the adoption and reformulation of these traditions; but there is no such thing as an original Germanic, and hence national, tradition, and such cannot be created."[18]

All the more important, therefore, is the attempt to preserve or to revivify the *religious tradition*.

The effort to create a *national religious tradition* finds expression among the extremes of political romanticism in a decisive struggle against Christianity and the construction of a Germanic paganism. The propagandistic effectiveness of this group, however, is small, since its goal too openly contradicts the acquired Christian disposition of the people, and its way of creating myths is too uninspired, literary, and fantastic to have any serious effect. Furthermore, there are no unified groups, whether priestly or lay, supporting it.

Much more effective is the actual expulsion of the Christian/prophetic element from the consciousness of the masses, who are bound to the myth of origin, and its replacement by faith in the nation as the highest human value. This seldom occurs explicitly, although a *rejection of the Old Testament* can be found even among official representatives of Christianity. More often this takes the implicit form of indifference to the church's proclamation and passionate devotion to the idea of the nation. What is sacred to the members of this movement is not what was sacred, for instance, to people of the Reformation period—religious truth and personal salvation. What is sacred to them is the nation, its freedom and power. The genuflection of the National Socialist party before the Protestant churches, therefore, does not signify that a secular movement here is seeking an arena in which to place itself under the judgment of the unconditional demand. Rather, it signifies that it wants what it considers holy to be confirmed by the ancient holy, and thus made acceptable to the adherents of the church. Catholicism up till now has refused to give this confirmation; Protestantism has done so, with certain limitations (which have no practical effect).[19]

This difference is rooted in the differing relationship of the two churches to the myth of origin. *Catholicism* has, in the hierarchy, a sociologically independent group that is able to preserve the religious tradition relatively undisturbed by the ebb and flow of historical movements. Just as earlier it gave no place to the Enlightenment's turning away from the origin, so today it makes no concessions to romanticism's return to the origin. For the romantic return ignores the myth of origin qualified by prophetism, as preserved by the church. It creates its own implicit or explicit myth, and this the church must reject. *Protestantism*, on the other hand, has no such fixed standpoint. The "Scriptures" have no fixed sociological expression. Protestantism, in principle, has no priesthood in the sense of the myth of origin. This means, however, that it lacks a counterweight to secular movements, all the more so since in Protestantism the laity are priests and the pastors also are laity. Protestantism is therefore sociologically dependent on the leading groups at any given time, whether the feudal lords or the bourgeoisie or the middle classes—be it by detour through the state or the economy or the party. So it comes about that its proclamation is either accommodated to the demands of the ruling groups, or else becomes so transcendent that it allows the social forces to work unhindered, and thereby serves their interests.[20] Just in this way, even if unknowingly and unintentionally, the Protestant churches today are performing a most important service to a movement that stands in sharpest contradiction to their own prophetic character. A further advantage to the return to the myth of origin is found in the fact that the churches are trying to expel once more the autonomous elements to which they had for a time allowed room, and which in Protestantism, in accordance with its principle, had achieved a decisive significance. Liberal Protestantism has been pressed to the edge of complete insignificance. Catholicism has pulled back into strict churchly heteronomy the free groups that it tolerated for a while. Corresponding to this sociologically is the destruction of the liberal form of civil society, and psychologically, the exhaustion of autonomous powers and the longing for new ties to father and mother that are found in the broadest circles.[21]

The return to the myth of origin shows its power also in the religious form of the return to primal revelation [*Uroffenbarung*]. However, the fact that the unbroken myth of origin contradicts the Christian principle means that it can win an enduring victory only if Christianity is wholly paganized and the Christian peoples reduced to the status of *fellaheen*. That this *can* happen is shown by the Christian East; that despite the most grievous catastrophe it *need not* happen is shown by the Christian West.[22]

4. The Cultural* Expression of Political Romanticism

The material powers and tendencies of political romanticism have been indicated. But they can unfold politically and have effect only through cultural and political articulation. The political struggle is impossible without the weapons of intellectual criticism and constructive thought. Therefore it is important to

---

* *Geistige,* also rendered in the text following as "spiritual" or "intellectual."—TRANS.

acquaint ourselves with these weapons, their significance, their appropriate uses, and the limits of their power.

One can arrange the forms of expression of political romanticism in stages according to the degree to which they are appropriate or inappropriate to what they are attempting to express. The farther from science and the closer to a. mythic view, the more appropriate is such an expression to the nature of political romanticism. In the realm in which the methods of mathematical natural science govern, directly or indirectly, political romanticism has no chance at all to express itself. Its chances begin with biology and anthropology, at best, but only to the extent that the philosophical elements in these disciplines are involved, not in the research as such. This is true also for sociology and history, although historiography does give room for romantic tendencies. In the cultural sciences and in philosophy, myth-of-origin thinking can express itself more directly, even if here it is still limited by the rational, scientific form of discourse. It is for this reason that poetry is more appropriate than philosophy to a consciousness oriented to the myth of origin. But poetry has a limit that makes it inappropriate as well: it only expresses what is. It can also express demands, but it cannot itself make demands or provide a basis for them. This, however, is just what political romanticism, as a political movement, must do. Therefore the most appropriate cultural forms of expression for this movement are those in which poetic or scientific elements are combined with priestly or prophetic ones (the former corresponding to conservative romanticism, the latter to revolutionary romanticism). Apocalyptic, which is ecstatic and revolutionary in nature, has proved at present to be the most effective cultural expression of political romanticism.

The strength of political romanticism does not lie in its scientific grounding. This indeed is not possible, since such romanticism necessarily falls into inner contradiction the moment it tries to assume scientific, i.e., rational, form. For this reason, in contrast to bourgeois liberalism and to proletarian socialism—both of which are rationally rooted—political romanticism has pro-

duced *no great theoreticians*, either in former times or in the
present. This striking deficiency is excused by political romanticism by appeal to the unfinished character of the movement, an
excuse that in fact confirms the point. But the great bourgeois
and socialist theoreticians stand precisely at the beginning of
their respective movements, which indeed, in essentials were
created by their efforts. That is impossible, however, for an antirational movement that wants to return to the origin. Theory, in
it, can at most be the description of what already exists, not
instructions for a reality yet to be created.

Since political romanticism gains access to the particular
sciences not through the methods of research but through their
philosophical presuppositions, we are justified in characterizing
first its philosophy, and then its effect upon the particular
sciences.

The myth of origin directs itself to the given in its original
form, prior to analysis or reformulation. In this we see already the
intuitive character of romantic philosophy. From Schelling's "intellectual intuition" down to the concept of intuition in the "philosophy of life" and phenomenology, there is a line of protest
against the analytical approach of modern bourgeois philosophy.
Intuition, for Schelling, does not dissolve things, does not subject
them to a law, does not want to dominate or shape them. It unites
with its object [*Gegenstand*], which is not something standing in
opposition [*Gegen-Stand*], not something to be manipulated, but
rather something to be drawn to oneself and taken into oneself.
Political romanticism tries to go behind the subject-object split
in all existing things, to break the power of analysis, to regain the
original unity, to accept rather than investigate, to "let be" rather
than to schematize.

Revolutionary romanticism appeals frequently to Nietzsche,
and not without justification. Nietzsche gave the highest rank to
the vital values, indeed to the animal level. In his struggle with
the bourgeois society of his time, he created most of the symbols of
political romanticism. He characterized and derided the victory
of the rational system as the victory of the "last man." He subordinated reason to life. He suggested that social revolution

amounts to nothing more than rebellion and resentment [*res-sentiment*] against the noble race. There is hardly an intellectual weapon of political romanticism that he did not forge, or at least sharpen. And yet he does not really belong to this movement. With passionate openness he admitted the heathen, anti-Christian character of these values and did not seek to give them an ideological cloak or a moral justification. He derided the nationalistic and anti-Semitic form of the blood-myth. In his depiction of the highest type there are elements that transcend animal values. Over against the befoggery of romantic thought he set the hardest, clearest knowledge, the most rational scientific method. Giving up one's autonomy would have been unthinkable for him, and a return to the origin, to the tie to father and mother, unbearable. He would never have recognized as the harbingers of the future the resentment-laden petit bourgeois groups that stand behind political romanticism. Only in one respect did he share the fate of political romanticism. He also came to grief on the contradiction of having to demand that which cannot be demanded, what either exists or does not exist. It is senseless to want to base the irrational on reason, or intuition on analytic concepts. But this is the compulsion and the contradiction of all romantic philosophy.

Nietzsche has receded into the background of contemporary consciousness. One somehow feels that it would be dangerous to invoke his name. Rather, there is the influence of Bergson in the *Action Française*, of Sorel and Pareto in Fascism, of Klages in the German youth movement, of the "philosophy of life" and phenomenology, above all of Spengler as the philosopher of history of a naturalistic form of political romanticism.

These figures have effects also beyond philosophy on into the realm of the sciences. Vitalism has gained new strength in the field of biology. The *idea of organism* has been elevated as the principle of a resolutely antiliberal social theory. The human being is understood from the standpoint of the body and its vitalistic powers. A racial theory with scientific claims is proffered. In the realm of economics, there is a quest for primal phenomena that can offer resistance to human efforts to alter things. Culture is banished into closed circles, and the idea of progress is ridiculed. History is changed into myth and spirit or intellect is equated with the fall into sin.

Here, assuredly, we see the whole contradiction of this form of thought. For it is spirit with which spirit is opposed; the disappearance of the concept of progress is considered to be progress; myth is verified by documents; and the organic society is to be achieved by force, through parties (Lat. *partes*, parts). The noble race makes itself the object of theory and practice, and the body receives its new dignity through the spirit, which wants to retire in favor of the body. Thought is to be negated by thinking, and action by acting. This is romantic theory and practice.

Less inappropriate than science and philosophy for political romanticism is *poetry*. Poetry makes no demands. It does not try to prove anything; it simply presents something. What is presented by poetry can certainly have a greater effect than any moral demand or scientific proof. Yet even this advantage of poetry is not without its limitations. Drama is inappropriate to the intention of political romanticism insofar as its real concern is with the elevation of humanity above the bondage of the myth of origin. Even if the ruin of humanity shows the superior power of the bonds of origin, this does not constitute a legitimation of the demand to remain in bondage. Wherever drama is alive, the myth of origin has been broken. And drama deals with the rightfulness and the tragedy of this break.

Epic is indeed what all romantic epochs long for, but can never realize. For epic can only be created by a consciousness that does not yet know the split between subject and object. On ground that has been thoroughly affected by rationalism, the novel takes the place of the epic. But the novel presupposes a distance from things—precisely what is to be overcome in the return to origin. In the novel, therefore, the dissolution of autonomy and longing for the origin can indeed find a direct expression, but the rediscovered origin itself cannot, through the novel, assume literary form.

Only lyric poetry can serve as a direct expression of the rediscovered origin. Here we must speak first and foremost of *Stefan George*, whose followers are already inclined to political romanticism by virtue of their interpretation of the idea of discipleship in terms of the myth of origin. But there is also in George the priestly element that is so important to our topic—the concept of grace, the esoterics of election, the cultic-hierarchical attitude. To be sure, even George does not escape the contradiction of romanticism. The priestly tradition of his circle is not an authentic tradition. It has been translated into the humanistic from the archaic sphere, and consequently has archaic traits. George's esoteric is grounded more strongly in intentionality and reflection, which are exoteric powers, than is appropriate to genuine esoterics. When the George school undertakes to translate myth from the poetic to the scientific sphere, we have the contradiction of a logos that is supposed to create mythos.

The Stefan George circle belongs in principle to the conservative type of political romanticism, corresponding to its priestly and esoteric elements. Revolutionary romanticism, on the other hand, needs a prophetic and exoteric factor in order to achieve victory. It is most interesting to note that political romanticism, since it has rejected true prophecy, creates for itself a form of expression which one might call *apocalyptic*, corresponding to an ancient literary type.[23] The difference is this: that the modern, secular apocalypse must appear in scientific form. Myth is believable on autonomous soil only in scientific guise. In this guise, however, it can become believable; and a political apocalypse can present itself as the most proper form of expression of political romanticism. Only in this way, not by virtue of its highly questionable scientific content, is the influence of periodicals like *Die Tat** understandable. Only in this way can the significance of the call for a "Third Reich" and the fantastic character of nearly all the programs and self-interpretations of revolutionary romanticism be understood. Science and poetry, united in revolutionary criticism and apocalyptic hope: this is the cultural form of expression of revolutionary romanticism. It is a political weapon of considerable, even if transient, effect.

---

* *See* above, p. xxxvi.—TRANS.

5. The Political Expression of Political Romanticism

The inner contradiction of political romanticism shows itself most clearly in its attitude toward political parties in general and to the existing parties in particular.

In bourgeois society, the *formation of parties* is the presupposition for winning political power. A political party presupposes the existence of autonomous conviction and processes of consensus formation amongst the general populace and its various subgroups. But autonomous processes of consensus formation are anathema to a myth-of-origin point of view. The latter is heteronomous and aristocratic. Therefore it can give birth to a political party only through a forced pseudomorphosis (apparent form). The conservative form of political romanticism can do this without danger, despite the inner contradiction, so long as the political dominance of the conservative groups makes the party a facade behind which quite other authoritative and aristocratic powers are operative.[24] Revolutionary romanticism does not have this option. Consequently it must destroy the form of the party from within and, while maintaining the fiction of a party, put in its place something completely different: a revolutionary fighting group that sees itself as an elite over against the people and through utter dedication forces its political will upon the people. Internally, it relies on authority and a rank-ordering of elites, all the way up to the Leader [*Führer*], in whose glorification the surrender of autonomy finds its strongest enthusiastic expression. Naturally, such a party can have no other goal than through its victory to make all parties disappear.

This basically antirational attitude, oriented to the myth of origin, does not prevent the parties of political romanticism from being the strongest and, in their revolutionary form, the final bulwark of the leading group of the rational system, namely, the capitalistic bourgeoisie. Just as the name "National Socialism" does not hinder the most important party of political romanticism at the present time from directing all its power to attacking socialism, so the apocalyptic pronouncements of doom which the intellectual groups of political romanticism direct at industrial society do not hinder the bearers of capitalistic power from using the new, supposedly anticapitalistic forms of social reconstruction to secure their own class dominance. These peculiarly *contradictory battle lines of political romanticism* can be explained, both socially and intellectually, by reference to the general situation of bourgeois society. The leading groups, especially of revolutionary romanticism, seek to counter the threat of their complete loss of power by depriving the rising proletariat of its power. Thereby they place themselves, in the class struggle, on the side of the ruling class. Conversely, the bourgeoisie, insofar as it has gained dominance, seeks to strengthen its position by giving play to myth-of-origin tendencies, thus feudalizing capitalistic rule at the cost of the proletariat. The decisive means employed to reach both ends is the idea of the national power-state. In this idea the myth of origin and capitalistic imperialism are best combined, serving to counteract the internationalizing effects of the bourgeois-rational system.

These factors are especially potent in Germany. The *German bourgeoisie* has never fought to actualize the democratic demands of its own principle. Rather, in idealistic fashion it removed them from the political sphere to that of pure inwardness. Both spiritually and socially, it accommodated itself to feudal forms, all the way down to its sliding without resistance into the catastrophe of the World War. By merging the military-conservative and the economic-imperialistic forms of the national idea, the bourgeoisie won over the leading groups of political romanticism. It deceived the middle classes through romantic and patriarchal notions, while in fact depriving them of economic power, and kept them from gaining any genuine feeling for democracy. When subsequently the revolution drew the consequences of the bourgeois principle, but at the same time presented demands to the bourgeoisie itself, the latter, in consequence of its involvement with prebourgeois strata and formations, could call on myth-of-origin thinking directly for assistance. It could go so far in this accommodation that for the sake of its own self-preservation it agreed to demands for national autarky that contradict its principle. It could forsake its own inner dynamic for the sake of a feudal stabilization. It could form a spiritual alliance with the ideology of the myth of origin, behave in a class-oriented and antiliberal manner, and even give up its spiritual autonomy for the sake of maintaining its class domination. Above all it could turn aside the discontent of the middle classes, who were economically disenfranchised through the developments after the World War, as all could see, and direct these feelings instead against the proletariat. *The fear of proletarianization was turned into a will to struggle against the proletariat.* This was possible because the proletariat, by virtue of the circumstances of the class struggle, was forced to carry through the bourgeois-democratic consequences of the rational system against the bourgeoisie and the prebourgeois strata allied with it, and to struggle against the dominance of capital, in which those strata participated in different degrees, or perhaps only seemed to participate.[25]

The inner contradiction of political romanticism in its social reality and in all its forms of expression follows necessarily from its character as a return to the origin under the presupposition of and by means of a society that has loosed itself from the origin. Here can be seen the effect of the relationship that we have described in principle between the two fundamental elements of human being and the two roots of political thought. Human beings cannot renounce being human. They must think; they must elevate being into consciousness; they must transcend the given. But when this has happened, there is no way back. *One cannot by thinking abolish thought; one cannot consciously reject consciousness.* But the attempt to do just this, if we understand it from its roots, is the meaning of political romanticism. Therein lies its lack of justification and its powerlessness over against the powers of bourgeois society. Its justification lies at another point than the one where political romanticism itself seeks for it; it lies precisely at the point where socialism also struggles against bourgeois society. It lies in the protest of human beings against the dehumanizing consequences of an exclusively rational system.

PART TWO:

THE PRINCIPLE OF

BOURGEOIS SOCIETY AND

THE INNER CONFLICT

OF SOCIALISM

CHAPTER 3

The Bourgeois Principle and the Proletariat

1. The Bourgeois Principle and Its Tensions

Western bourgeois society is the product of a double break with the bond of origin: the prophetic and the humanistic. The prophetic break occurred in Protestantism, most radically and most effectively in Calvinism. The humanistic break occurred in the Enlightenment and (after overcoming the opposing movements) in the positivism and liberalism of the nineteenth century. In Protestantism, Western consciousness freed itself from the medieval bonds of origin supported and protected by the priesthood; in the Enlightenment, it freed itself from the heteronomy of the absolutism, both religious and political, that had characterized the period of transition. The prophetic background of the bourgeois spirit in the West expresses itself in the active, world-transforming will which differentiates this spirit from most forms of Greek thought. The portrayal of bourgeois society and its world historical significance in the *Communist Manifesto* depicts, in a most penetrating way, the uniqueness of this phenomenon in all recorded history. *Western bourgeois society, viewed from the standpoint of universal history, is an attack on the myth of origin and the bond of origin everywhere on earth.* It is the proclamation and realization of an autonomous this-worldliness even for the most remote, most mythbound human groups. Through the triumphant spread of its principle it has established a world dominion which no one on earth can completely elude. Wherever

technology and capital are at work, the spirit of Western bourgeois society is active.[1]

*Its principle is the radical dissolution of all conditions, bonds,
and forms related to the origin into elements that are to be rationally mastered, and the rational assemblage of these elements
into structures serving the aims of thought and action.* Goal setting takes the place of concern for being, the creation of tools
replaces the contemplation of intrinsic values. The bourgeoisie, as
an alien force, tames the arbitrary powers of existence; this it
does by subjecting them to its own ends. And the way it tames
them is by objectification and analysis. In every origin there is an
element of the unconditioned. The wholly conditioned, that
which has become merely a thing, no longer bears any marks of
the origin. Therefore total objectification is the abolishing of all
reference to origin in an entity, its complete profanization. The
spirit of bourgeois society is the spirit of a human group that,
after cutting every bond of origin, subjugates an objectified world
to its own purposes.

Objectification involves nature as well as human society. The
analysis of nature leads to its reduction to a practical system of
mathematical functions, and the utilization of functionally calculable elements in the service of technical and economic goals.
The analysis of society leads to the factoring out of individual
persons, driven by instinct and choice, as the elements out of
which every society is built. By manipulating the drive-mechan-
isms of individuals and of masses, one can achieve a rational
mastery of social processes. Thus, here also a complete objectification occurs: by virtue of the prediction of his reactions, the
human person, as a psychologically and sociologically determined
unit, is rendered serviceable for the achievement of certain goals.
The bonds of origin are severed, both within the life of the
individual and in the social group.

The analysis and mastery of nature and of society presuppose a
power that exercises mastery. In this connection the following
questions arise: Who can exercise such rule, and how is such
domination possible in both nature and society? How is it possible that human intelligence can know nature and bring it into

its service through this knowledge? And how is it possible for society to be rationally structured? *Who is to be responsible for the structuring of society, and what guarantee is there that it will be done rationally?* This question presupposes that the powers of origin that had exercised an unquestioned dominion have lost their power. It is at this point that the problem of how nature can be grasped through human knowledge and how society can be constructed through human activity is of greatest urgency. We encounter here the *subject-object problem*, that great catalyst of Western philosophy, and, in strict correlation with it, the *problem of freedom and authority*, the catalyst of bourgeois political thought. Epochs that are close to the myth of origin do not know either of these antinomies. Rather, they live in terms of an original unity of subject and object (a formulation which is unavoidable but inadequate, because it presupposes a split); and they live in terms of primal structures of authority that at the same time offer a graduated system of freedoms.

Two answers are possible, and two have been given, to these questions raised by the bourgeois principle. The first proceeds from the object, whether nature or the social forces of production, and affirms that nature gives itself to human sense experience in such a way that a knowledge of nature occurs that is sufficient for mastery over it (the epistemology of positivism). It affirms, further, that the free flow of human productive forces will lead inevitably to a rational formation of society, whether in the realm of culture (tolerance), economics (liberalism), or politics (theory of majority rule). It believes, thus, that an entity, as soon as it can unfold in freedom from the powers of origin, will arrive through a *natural harmony* at the fulfillment of being. Back of this liberal idea of harmony stands the religious belief in the unity and goodness of the world. The motto *"Laissez faire, laissez aller"* has its roots in piety.

The second answer proceeds from the subject. It is based on the conviction that leaving the individual elements of nature and society to themselves will never lead to a rational knowledge of nature or a rational formation of society. The subject is the bearer of reason, in the sense that the spirit gives nature its laws (Kant) and that the central government rationally directs and shapes all aspects of society, bringing the productive powers of every kind —spiritual, economic, and political—into effective harmony. *Nature and society are to be subjected to human reason.* The freedom of the individual must be circumscribed by an overarching law. Insofar as this tendency does not appear in the guise of the myth of origin as an enlightened absolutism, but rather adopts the liberal premise, one can call it democratic (in contrast to consistent) liberalism. One thus can speak of an antithesis, in the social sphere, of equality and freedom. But as soon as one employs the word "democracy" in this somewhat antiliberal sense, it is necessary to place the accent on the second part of the Greek word, i.e. on "rule."

For liberalism and democracy in fact belong very closely together. Each is at work within the other; and in spite of the sharpest tensions that may arise between them, they can never be separated. In every democracy, however centralized and controlled it may be, the fundamental assumption is liberal: namely, that the individual is the source of the authority to which he subjects himself. On the basis of natural right, the individual shares in determining who should represent and execute the overarching requirements of reason. As an individual, one is the object of an education that has as its basic presupposition one's own freedom and capacity for rational thought. As the bearer of an indeterminate power of productivity, the individual will be taken into account by those responsible for planning. In a system bound to the myth of origin, on the other hand, the individual neither is asked for his opinion, nor is he educated in terms of a faculty of reason that is equally active in every individual, nor regarded as a quantum of productive power. Thus we see that liberalism, which is the element that frees humanity from the bond of origin, is active also in a structured democracy.

On the other hand, even the most extreme liberalism, if it has not turned into a form of utopian anarchism, requires something to assure the unhindered working of the forces of production and the untrammeled development of intellectual and political freedom. Such a guarantee can be given only by a central authority that has the power to repel whatever might tend to limit, inwardly or outwardly, the natural development. One cannot say in advance to what extent this authority might have to intervene in order to overcome disturbances of the natural harmony. In some cases its interventions must go so far that the liberal principle is almost eliminated. This happens especially when the disturbances come from without, when a threat to the nation makes dictatorial measures necessary.

By virtue of their common belief in harmony, *the interpenetration of liberalism and democracy* is yet further deepened. Liberalism believes in a natural harmony which comes to pass through the free play of the productive forces. Democracy does not believe in *natural harmony*; it does believe, however, that nature can be subjugated to reason. It believes in a *metaphysical harmony* which is certain to prevail in the historical process. Nature is knowable, and can be put into the service of humanity, because the categories of the human mind are the elements that give nature its structure. Society can be rationally shaped because the human race is involved in a process of education toward reason, the goal of which will somehow finally be reached. This belief in harmony, whether in the one form or the other, is the most profound principle of the Western Enlightenment, though it often remains unrecognized.[2] It is the principle that has given the Enlightenment its optimism and has given bourgeois society its world historical power. *If the belief in harmony is shaken, the bourgeois principle is shaken.* The bourgeois principle cannot be protected from this shock by giving up the liberal belief in natural harmony, while maintaining the belief in a metaphysical harmony to be achieved through human action. Without the liberal element, democracy's expectation of progress is nothing more than a belief in miracles. For without the liberal premise, democracy cannot explain how, out of the arbitrariness of all individuals, a power can emerge that educates toward reason and achieves the reasonable. It cannot do without the concept of natural harmony in its description either of the individual or of society. If it nevertheless wants to give up this concept, it is compelled to fall back on prebourgeois, origin-related elements.

BIRMINGHAM UNIVERSITY LIBRARY

Sociologically speaking, the bourgeoisie, shattered in its economic and political self-confidence, is constrained either to put the blame for the shattering of harmony on the disturbance of *laissez faire* by the powers of origin (those of a political, and especially national, character)[3] or it must find security in a return to pre-bourgeois feudal structures. Both strategies are being pursued at the present time, the former as yet only in theoretical discussions by small groups, the latter as the path actually followed by advanced capitalistic powers.

2. *The Leading Groups and the Limits of the Bourgeois Principle*

The active bearers of the bourgeois spirit are the groups that are alienated from the myth of origin by their social situation: the intellectuals (excluding the clergy), as champions of inner autonomy; public officials, insofar as they represent the controlling reason of the state; employees of higher rank, who with the elimination of the small businessman through the concentration of capital have achieved increasing importance; the workers, who have been wrenched loose from their ties to home and to the transcendent and have become mere means toward the achievement of economic goals and possessors of "labor power," viewed as a commodity; wholesale merchants, for whom entities are merchandise and therefore things, and who lose all ties to the land by an essentially unrestricted form of commercial exchange; the industrial entrepreneurs, as agents of economic autonomy; the managers of finance capital, who have a function in directing the market which is devoid of every bond of origin.

Liberalism prevails, in bourgeois society, among the groups that require the free play of forces for their development, and for whom the idea of harmony provides justification for their unlimited economic aspirations, i.e., among individual entrepreneurs in commerce, industry, and finance. When commercial interests are combined into power groups, however, the idea of harmony becomes merely an ideology serving to protect the power structures from governmental interference and from socialist efforts to place limitations on them. Only certain groups that are less susceptible to concentration then still represent genuine liberalism: for example, light manufacturing as opposed to heavy industry, or private bankers as opposed to the major banks. Among the large cartels, the Enlightenment's paradoxical concept of harmony is being more and more transformed into the feudal, stratified concept of organism espoused by political romanticism. *This is the way from liberalism to the new feudalism.*

Democratic tendencies are found whenever belief in natural harmony retreats in favor of the rational drive to shape reality, i.e., among public officials, who as representatives of the overarching unity of the state are inclined toward restraining the free play of forces and the irresponsible forms of domination that result from it. The intellectuals usually affirm liberalism for the sake of their own autonomy, but because of their lack of economic power they are prone to antiliberal tendencies. Their opposition to liberalism, when allied with the struggle of the proletariat, can even lead to a renunciation of intellectual autonomy; this indeed is a very frequent occurrence today. The proletariat, i.e., the masses that as a result of free competition have become mere objects of the social process, are clearly antiliberal. As such they stand, to be sure, on the soil of bourgeois society, but they are, at the same time, the living contradiction of it. The proletarian struggle against liberalism is a struggle against the bourgeois class rule that was erected with the help of liberalism. Its struggle for democracy is a struggle to see that all have an equal share in social power and economic profits. In this struggle it can happen that the liberal element that is inherent in the democratic order is sacrificed. Because of doubt that it is possible under the established patterns of domination to achieve democracy by democratic means, a transitional *dictatorship of the proletariat* is demanded, and consequently a partial sacrifice of the idea of equality. When this final step is taken, the intrabourgeois opposition to bourgeois society comes to coincide with the revolutionary form of political romanticism, just as the intrabour-

geois development out of bourgeois society, namely, feudalization, comes to coincide with the conservative form of political
romanticism.[4]

These splits within bourgeois society and the transitions to pre-
and postbourgeois structures were implicit in its existence from
the beginning. The bourgeois principle is a dynamic, formative
principle, not a static, supportive one. It dissolves things and
brings them together in a new way, but it does not create anything original. It presupposes what has been created, and makes
use of it for its own purposes. Thus autonomy lives out of the
substance of the myth of origin, which it transforms into the
human; the dynamic of industrialism lives out of the preindustrial
sectors which it conquers; democratic rule lives out of the origin-
related phenomenon of subjection to the state not for the sake of
the state's purposes but on account of its power of being. Consequently, in order to be able *to be* at all, bourgeois society must
allow itself to be supported by a reality that it does not form, but
which it finds already in existence. It must unite itself, ideologically and socially, with the supporting powers of origin. It cannot
implement its principle alone; it cannot make it into a universal
principle. Rather, it must allow it to function as a *critical principle* in a world which is already given. Thus is explained the
remarkable fact that bourgeois society in all countries has abjured
any consistent implementation of its own principle. This is to be
explained not simply ideologically, in terms of the limitations of
its external political power, but rather in terms of a proper instinct for the fact that the bourgeois principle by itself cannot be
the basis for existence. It is *a corrective, not a normative*, principle. Thus it was in the relation between the prophets and the
priests: prophetism had to appeal to the primal revelation of the
priests, and had to express itself in a priestly manner. The relation
between Protestantism and Catholicism is similar: Protestantism
was able to become a church only by virtue of the Catholic
elements.

This law applies also to bourgeois society. Thus *classicism* is to
be understood as the attempt to appropriate the substance of the
myth of origin in an autonomous form. From a sociological per-

spective, classicism is the union of active feudal powers with the advocates of the bourgeois principle. Similarly, *idealism* is to be understood as the attempt to derive a world of meaning and value from reason, the supreme norm of the bourgeois spirit, and to conserve the values of origin in the unity of a rational system. Sociologically speaking, this means the replacement of the priest-hood as the guardian of primal revelation with autonomous intel-lectuals as discoverers of universal reason. So, too, *historicism* is to be understood as the attempt of the bourgeoisie to find an authentic tradition, tracing itself to cultures which are bound to the origin. Sociologically, this signifies the preservation of older social groups under the aegis of the bourgeoisie; psychologically, it is the preservation of the deeper spiritual levels under the hegemony of the conscious mind. The maintenance of *religious forms of life* is to be understood in a similar manner, whether in the guise of impeccable propriety, as in England, or in terms of the problem of autonomous reason, as in Germany. Materialism and atheism are rejected by the victorious bourgeois society, as it attempts to give itself the sanctity and power of transcendence in spite of its basic immanence. Sociologically speaking, this means the admission into bourgeois society of strata bound to primal revelation—while guarding, to be sure, against any attempt of orthodoxy to interfere with the autonomous progress of the bourgeoisie. Psychologically speaking, it means a splitting of the person into one level of rational consciousness and another of prerational religious feeling. The frequent *criticism of the bour-geois principle by the bourgeoisie itself*, the turning toward the irrational, the living, the depth dimension, to undisturbed nature, is to be understood similarly. Yet none of these self-negations is really a radical negation. They almost never have practical con-sequences, since they occur with the help of the very principle that is to be negated—critical reason. But neither do they amount to mere sham, since they derive from the feeling that without these powers the bourgeois principle cannot exist.

Finally, the same is to be understood of the grandest effort of this kind, that of *bourgeois nationalism*. The powers inherent in the idea of the nation, which are very closely related to the myth of origin, are utilized in the struggle for the interests of the national bourgeois economic groups. Domestically, opposition to the domination of these groups is condemned as unpatriotic.[5] Internationally, the economic struggle against them is interpreted as a struggle against the nation. Thus the bourgeoisie, with the help of the idea of the nation, succeeds in overcoming its political opponents at home, in enlisting in its service the prebourgeois forces that are still bound to the origin, and in reducing competition in the world market, either by political suppression of the competing nations or by barring their products (imperialism or autarky).

All these things have been interpreted, and opposed, as ideology—i.e., as the *false consciousness* the bourgeoisie has concerning itself. It is not a false consciousness, however, but a true consciousness of the limits of the bourgeois principle and the impossibility of its standing alone without a supportive prebourgeois substance. The intellectual and political ties between the bourgeois and the prebourgeois world are based on this consciousness, which corresponds to the limits that are inherent in any bourgeois deployment of power. Here is an expression of the fact that being is always and everywhere more decisive than consciousness, that the original is more decisive than what has been shaped by human effort.

This tendency becomes romantic only when the bourgeois principle seeks to abolish itself. Political romanticism truly is a false consciousness, because it does not recognize what meanwhile has transpired: the victory of the bourgeois principle, which can be reversed only through its collapse, not through nostalgic longing. Stated in economic terms, in a thoroughly rationalized market economy, the collapse of the rational market must result in the collapse of the society that lives on the basis of this market. The way from being to consciousness, from origin to structure, cannot be reversed without the destruction of the society that has undergone this development. Political romanticism is a false consciousness, whereas the union of prebourgeois and bourgeois elements in the whole history of Western civilization rests on a true consciousness of the effective power and effective limits of the bourgeois principle.

3. The Radicalization and the Shattering of the Bourgeois Principle in the Class Struggle

To the extent that the bourgeois principle, on one hand, allies itself with the powers of the myth of origin and thus is in danger of being suppressed or expelled by reactionary romanticism, groups arise, on the other hand, that press for the radical breakthrough of the liberal and democratic tendencies that are implicit in the principle. This *bourgeois radicalism*, as it first appears, attacks not only the romantic reactionary powers by which the bourgeoisie has been smothered, but also the forms of life and spirit in which the bourgeoisie has deliberately united itself with the prebourgeois groups. It attempts to achieve a standpoint of pure immanence, opposing idealism and the remnants of priestly bonds. In so doing, it does not shrink from materialistic consequences, indeed, it resolutely forwards the objectification of the world and of humanity. (In Germany, Feuerbach and Strauss are typical examples of this.) Bourgeois radicalism seeks to abolish the semifeudal forms of rule which the conservative bourgeoisie has embraced or to which it had to resign itself, in favor of unrestricted democracy. This was the meaning of the bourgeois revolution of 1848 in Germany. It attempted to free all strata of society from the bonds of origin, both spiritually and materially, by raising the idea of progress to the status of an ontological and ethical principle. This was the aim of the bourgeois *Fortschrittspartei* (Progressive Party)* in Germany. Bourgeois radicalism attempted, through a radical work of enlightenment, to bring to rational consciousness the levels of the psyche and of society not yet dominated by the conscious mind. This was the purpose of the enlightenment of the people by the popularization of scientific knowledge. It sought to free the idea of the nation from the

* Full name *Deutsche Fortschrittspartei,* literally "German Progress Party." Founded in Prussia in 1861, it worked for the strengthening of parliamentary democracy and for German unity under Prussian leadership, while opposing most of Bismarck's policies. Merged into the *Deutsche Freisinnige Partei* in 1884. Its tradition later found embodiment in the *Fortschrittliche Volkspartei* and, after World War I, in the *Deutsche Demokratische Partei.*—TRANS.

elements of power politics; it was antimilitaristic and pacifist. These were the roots of the struggle of the German liberals against Bismarck and the Prussian military budget. Thus bourgeois radicalism attempts to draw the consequences of the bourgeois principle in all areas, consequences from which the increasingly conservative bourgeoisie shrinks back. In the idea of progress, the clearest symbol of this tendency, the idea of harmony found in the nineteenth century its most fruitful realization.

Socialism, in its origins, goes hand in hand with this bourgeois radicalism. The concern for a full realization of the bourgeois principle rather than its restriction by the ruling bourgeoisie grows out of the proletarian situation. But something else grows out of it, too: the experience that the bourgeois belief in harmony and in progress stands in total contradiction to the proletarian situation. The bourgeois principle as applied by liberalism does not lead to a harmonious society characterized by steady progress and contentment, but to crisis, class rule, and class struggle.[6] The proletariat does not experience harmony, but *disharmony*. And on the basis of this experience, in which it becomes directly aware of its proletarian existence, it separates itself from bourgeois radicalism and becomes as much opposed to the radical as to the conservative bourgeoisie.

The liberal element of the bourgeois principle is subordinated to the democratic element; the former is disregarded during the period of class rule. A balance of freedom and equality is expected to appear only in the classless society. The harmony that liberalism, in its original or progressive form, believes it sees in the present is postponed to the end-time, when society reaches fulfillment. At present, disharmony dominates; it is too deeply and necessarily grounded in the social situation to be overcome by progress. Only through the compulsory power of the whole over against all individuals, that is, through a centralized democracy with a real power of rulership, can the fragmentation of social unity be overcome. The free play of forces is to be replaced by *deliberate planning*. The authorities without accountability that arise on liberal soil are to be replaced by a democratically based, accountable, central authority.

Thus socialism has shifted from the liberal to the democratic element of the bourgeois principle. But now it falls into the same difficulties as did the bourgeoisie when its liberal foundations were shaken. If the liberal element is excluded, democracy is compelled to support itself by reaching back to the prebourgeois feudal powers. Reason, the central principle of planning and education, must be supported by a power that is capable of desiring and establishing socialism. As long as socialism rests on democratic presuppositions, it must acknowledge that this power comes into being through the free decisions of all individuals—in practice, through majority vote. The possibility of gaining majority support for socialism is thwarted, however, by the reality of class rule. Bourgeois class rule is based on the alliance of the bourgeoisie with prebourgeois groups. Over against this combination, the numerical limitations of the industrial proletariat make the attainment of a socialist majority to all intents and purposes impossible. The political, financial, and intellectual resources that the powers of capitalism have at their disposal hinder the enlightenment and education of the nonproletarian masses along socialist lines. If the domination of bourgeois society is successfully shaken, however, by virtue of political catastrophes (defeat in war, economic crises), it has other means to counteract the effects of socialist influence: the economic undermining of the power of governments influenced by socialism (inflation); the applying of pressure by other states (capitalistic wars of intervention); the pitting of military against civil authority (the *coup de main* against Prussia*); the quiet opposition of the middle and lower levels of the civil service (which stem, for the most part, from prebourgeois groups); but above all, the employment of the idea of the nation to strengthen all the powers related to the origin that have been co-opted by the bourgeoisie, even when this tactic results in the support of an apparently antibourgeois, revolutionary movement (National Socialism). *In the face of the split between classes, the democratic belief in harmony as held by the bourgeoisie is shattered; in the face of bourgeois class rule, the*

---

* *See* Introduction, note 2.—TRANS.

democratic belief in harmony as held by socialism collapses.

Socialism's only alternative is to enlist in the struggle forces that can be characterized as powers of origin, the affirmation of which will mean the surrender of the democratic premise and thereby of the bourgeois principle. This takes place under the *symbolic concept of the dictatorship of the proletariat.* This concept is both symbolic and ambiguous. Dictatorship, in the strict sense of the word, occurs only in a democratic setting, whether it be a small group (such as a group of aristocrats of equal power) or the entire people that submits to a dictator. What is decisive is that this submission occurs as a free choice and is to prevail only for a limited time, so that the dictator is both installed and removed in a democratic way. Where these presuppositions are absent, a dictatorship in the strict sense of the word cannot be said to obtain; it is, rather, a revolutionary elevation of a particular power group over the existing power structures. To be sure, there may be an intent, which even forms part of the theory, that the victorious power group (e.g., the proletariat after the defeat of class rule) should give up its position of power. But the victorious group is in no way compelled to do so. After its victory, it is not subordinate to democracy, but rather democracy is subordinate to it. In this situation it has the same position as a military or other power group intruding from without, and the question of how it exploits its position is left completely to its own discretion.

The concept of the dictatorship of the proletariat contains yet another ambiguity. The proletariat as a whole obviously cannot exercise the dictatorship. Seizure of power is possible only by the use of picked troops who are ready for sacrifice; likewise the maintenance of power is possible only through an elite of the victorious proletariat. Thereby a differentiation arises that favors tendencies related to the myth of origin and leads of necessity to a new feudalization, even though in a different form than pre-bourgeois feudalism.

The renunciation of the democratic principle in the class struggle, the necessity—which is becoming ever clearer—to secure dominion despite the lack of a majority, introduces a severe conflict between present and future into socialism. The bourgeois idea of harmony is abandoned for the present. Even the proletarian struggle cannot in any way rely on it. But if socialism has surrendered the heart of the bourgeois principle with respect to all reality up to the present, can it really maintain the bourgeois principle at all? Is an interpretation of the world warranted that so contradicts experience that it must renounce its essential claim both for the present and for the past? Can an interpretation of the world that does not involve a belief in miracles expect something in the future that contradicts all previous knowledge of reality? *Can socialism be the fulfillment of the bourgeois principle when at the same time it is the expression of its destruction?* Must not the struggle against bourgeois society question the bourgeois principle itself? Does the socialist principle contain elements that fundamentally transcend the bourgeois principle, and that derive from the other root of political thought, the one from which political romanticism derives its power?

These questions compel us to undertake an exact analysis of socialism in its contemporary form.

4. The Proletariat and Socialism

The opposition to the bourgeois principle on the basis of the bourgeois principle arises from the proletariat. Insofar as socialism is the expression of this opposition, it is bound to the existence of the proletariat; insofar as it seeks to eliminate proletarian existence, and thus the opposition of classes, it transcends the proletarian situation and includes all of society. *Socialism has both a particular and a universal aspect.* These two aspects belong together; they cannot be separated. To consider only the universal aspect is to make socialism a general ethical and political idea for which there is no leading group. To consider socialism only in its particularity is to deny its capability of overcoming the class situation and thereby proletarian existence; this reduces socialism to being the *ressentiment* of a suppressed class. Socialism can be properly understood only in terms of the interaction between its particular and universal elements.

Socialism is an expression of the proletarian situation. Its principle is the power of the proletarian movement. This particular aspect must be strictly adhered to, and must not become weakened in an idealistic manner. The proletariat has come to consciousness in socialism; it is constituted as a proletariat by socialism. For "proletariat" means more than a mass of people who are affected by a common fate. It means a class that is conscious of itself as a class. It is socialism, to be sure, that has given it this consciousness. The unanswerable question as to where the proletariat begins and ends is falsely conceived. The concept of the proletariat is not a strictly empirical concept that encompasses a specific number of persons and unambiguously defines their particular characteristics. Rather *the proletariat is an "ideal type,"* i.e., a concept that describes a social structure according to its decisive characteristics without regard to whether this structure is immediately and purely evident in experience. *The proletariat, furthermore, is an existential concept,* i.e., one which cannot be derived from the consciousness of one who is only a spectator. What the proletariat is can only be understood from within the proletarian struggle, and by taking a stand within this struggle. "Proletariat," at its deepest level, is a polemical concept [*Kampfbegriff*]. The proletarian struggle, however, is the socialist struggle. Therefore the proletariat is just as much a creation of socialism as socialism is a creation of the proletariat. They are reciprocally related. Socialism is the self-consciousness of the proletariat, and thus is its basis, since the establishment of human social being is always, at the same time, the establishment of a consciousness in which this being fulfills itself. For human being is conscious being.

The strict relationship between socialism and the proletariat ought not be taken to imply that at first there were only the chaotic masses, on which socialism then superimposed its ideology; as though *intellectuals* and *agitators* brought socialism to the uprooted masses from outside. Neither intellectuals nor agitators would have been able to create the socialistic movement if socialism were not a genuine expression of the proletarian masses. Intellectuals and agitators cannot create any movement at all

unless they give expression to an existence that cries out, inde-
pendently, for expression and fulfillment. It is therefore incorrect
to distinguish a proletarian socialism from some other sort of
socialism.[7] If the connection between socialism and the proletariat is broken, they both cease to be what they are. There can
still be movements that seek a new order of justice. But they are
not *socialist*. It is therefore impossible to understand socialism, its
reality and its principle, unless one begins with the proletariat.
On the other hand, the proletarian situation cannot be described
without including the socialist self-consciousness through which
the proletarian situation is defined as proletarian. So close is the
connection and so fundamental is the particular aspect of socialism.

Socialism, however, would not have had the power to give the
proletariat its self-consciousness, and thereby its basis as the
proletariat, if it had lacked the other dimension, the universal.
For in the universal tendency of socialism is expressed the will of
the proletariat to move beyond itself—not in the sense of an
upward mobility into the bourgeois class, but in the sense of a
new form of human being and of society as a whole. The symbolic name for this form of being is *classless society*. Through this
desire and this expectation, the proletariat places itself in historical contexts that far transcend its particular form of being. It
stands directly on the soil of the bourgeois culture of the Christian West. It carries within itself the religious and secular history
of the West and has been formed by it, just as the bourgeois and
prebourgeois groups have been. Thereby it is closed, both in
being and in consciousness, to non-Christian possibilities as they
are realized, for example, in Asia. The proletariat in the strict
sense, and therefore socialism, will be conceivable on Asiatic soil
only when Christian humanism has conquered the peoples of
Asia. It corresponds to the advanced state of development of
Japan that there a movement has been able to maintain itself that
is a close equivalent of European socialism or Communism.

Christian humanism, as the background of proletarian existence, is expressed in the interaction and tension of the different
elements that it carries within itself: *Christianity* in its different

periods and churches, Greek *humanism*, and Jewish *prophetism*. The socialist principle contains all these elements within itself. It is not merely a general demand standing over against history, but neither is it merely a special empirical principle, the description of a unique historical phenomenon. Rather, it is a particular principle that at the same time expresses human being in general. It is rooted in a primordial human element: the demand, the transcendent, the expectation of the new. This is its universality. It has been formed historically in the development of the Judeo-Christian tradition, down to the Christian humanism of bourgeois society; and it has come to specific realization in the Western proletariat. The universal and the particular element—human being [*Sein*] and proletarian existence [*Dasein*]—therefore do not stand alongside each other in an unrelated way. They are related through a history that reaches back to the origins of life, and which leads via Christianity and humanism to socialism.

In spite of the reciprocity of socialism and the proletariat, tensions can arise between the universal and the particular elements. From the side of the universal element, demands can be made which would absorb the particular element. Socialism would become a sociologically rootless general idea, thereby losing its historical power. This is the danger of an *intellectual socialism*, which the proletariat rightly has always opposed. For such an intellectual socialism is derived from the bourgeois situation and its type of political thinking. It seeks from this standpoint to plan a coming order of justice by leaping over the proletarian situation. Whatever such a plan may be called, and however it may be regarded, it is in any case not socialist. The struggle against utopian socialism is based on the inseparable connection between socialism and the proletariat that Marx has demonstrated, a connection that must not be severed by the universal tendency.

But just as little should the universal character of socialism be given up for the sake of this solidarity. This, too, has been a continual danger ever since the victory of Marxism amongst the German proletariat. At present it is the greater danger, and it has already had ominous effects in the political realm. The opposition to Marxism in Germany has among other, profounder causes, also the fact that groups inclined toward socialism cannot accept the complete particularization that adheres to it by virtue of its connection with the proletariat. An emphasis on the universal element which is implicit in the proletariat's desire to abolish itself as a proletariat will bring to the side of socialism strong forces that are now forced into opposition to it. The present study can be understood as an effort *to work out the universal element of socialism without giving up the particular element.*

CHAPTER 4

The Inner Conflict of Socialism

Introduction: The Inner Conflict of Proletarian Existence

Proletarian existence is characterized by a conflict that is grounded in the relationship of the proletariat to bourgeois society. *Conflict is not contradiction.* In a contradiction, there is a subjective, accidental, arbitrary element in that which contradicts itself. Contradictions require the surrender of that which is contradictory. A genuine contradiction, as for example in political romanticism, compels one to decide in terms of either/or. In the case of a conflict, this is not so. Conflict is not rooted in the knowing subject, in the accidental and arbitrary, but in the thing itself. This difference is expressed by adding the word "inner." An inner conflict is one that derives from the law of the thing itself. This is the meaning of the Greek term made famous by Kant, "antinomy," that is, "lawful opposition." An inner conflict, an antinomy, cannot be removed by a movement within the knowing subject, by abandoning contradictory thinking or acting. An antinomy can only be resolved by changing the structure from which the inner conflict necessarily proceeds. Our analysis of political romanticism has demonstrated the *contradiction* on which it must run aground. Our analysis of the bourgeois principle has demonstrated the inner *conflict* of socialism, which can only be resolved by socialism's arriving at a new form of itself. But because of the close connection between socialism and the proletariat, a new form is possible only if proletarian existence is transformed at the same time.

To begin with, the proletariat is nothing but a product of bourgeois society and its formation of the world and of society. It is the result of the complete objectification of all existing things in nature and society through the domination of the bourgeois principle. In the proletariat, all bonds to the myth of origin have been completely broken. The individual is left entirely to himself. Immediately supporting powers such as soil, blood, group, and community are lacking. While the bourgeoisie disclaimed for itself the radical implications of its own principle and allied itself with prebourgeois forces, it abandoned the proletariat completely to the dynamic of this principle. The prebourgeois support of bourgeois class rule, whether by means of religious, nationalistic, or patriarchal ideologies, in no way implies a change in the class situation of the proletariat. Rather, such support signals a reinforcement of class rule and an intensifying of the class struggle. It implies an attenuation of the dynamic of bourgeois society, and thus a postponement of the proletariat's prospects for overthrowing class rule. Consequently, in the class struggle the proletariat is forced to fight against the prebourgeois principle and for the bourgeois principle—not, however, in order to support the latter, but to destroy it! Thus arises the conflict expressed in the fact that the proletariat, as a class within bourgeois society, lives on the resources of the bourgeois society against which it struggles. It must live on these resources. For its class situation is precisely this: always to be only an object, never a subject, within bourgeois society; that is, to be robbed of a principle of life of its own.[8]

If this side of proletarian existence were the only one, there would be no such thing as socialism. The proletariat (which then would not be a proletariat in the proper sense) would bow to class rule without resistance. It would have no strength to say "no" to that from which it lives. It must get this strength from elsewhere. The existence of socialism presupposes that the proletariat is able to resist the bourgeois principle as a whole. This means it must carry within itself elements of the first root of political thought, i.e., powers of origin. For it is precisely with their help that the bourgeoisie has consolidated its rule. *The proletariat must deny that power by which it struggles against the bourgeois principle, namely, the power of the origin. And it must affirm that which it seeks to destroy, namely, the bourgeois principle. This is the inner conflict in which it stands.* This is the reason for the deep inner problematic of every manifestation of socialism; it is the reason for the impotence and atrophy especially of German socialism. The proletarian situation would be clear and unambiguous if it were only the radical realization of the bourgeois principle, the complete rationalization of the social process in the sense of the bourgeois belief in harmony. But this it cannot be, since the class struggle means precisely the historical refutation of the belief in harmony. The bourgeois principle as a whole must therefore be attacked. Again, the situation would be clear and unambiguous if the attack could be waged consistently on the basis of the prebourgeois elements, the powers of origin. But this, too, is impossible because of the alliance of the bourgeoisie and prebourgeois powers, entered into by the bourgeoisie not in order to limit or eliminate its principle but to strengthen and maintain its class rule. Therefore, the proletariat, in constant ambiguity vis-à-vis the powers of origin, must struggle against the alliance of bourgeois society and prebourgeois forces. The burden of its struggle and perhaps the tragedy of its fate is rooted in this ambiguity. A reversal of this tragedy is only possible if the proletariat is led to an awareness of its situation and makes a clear decision for the powers of origin, while rejecting the forces of origin that have become bourgeois, together with the bourgeois principle itself. This, basically, is the "socialist decision" that is demanded of German socialism. Our demonstration of the inner conflict in all the manifestations of socialism will justify this demand.

1. The Inner Conflict of Socialist Belief

The inner conflict of socialism that results from the antinomy of proletarian existence can be seen, first of all, in socialist belief. Socialism shares the belief in the possibility of rational control of the world, and in the possibility of creating, through the human capacity to know and to shape the external world, an economic and social order that is adequate to the natural purposes of all people. But since socialism does not believe that this order is already present as an invisibly working harmony, but rather that the untrammeled operation of the forces of production, as urged by the belief in harmony, results in fact in disharmony, socialism must direct its faith toward a future that stands in complete contradiction to the present. It must recast the belief in harmony into an eschatological expectation. The democratic idea of progress cannot help in this task, since belief in progress is a version of belief in harmony. *If socialism expects the coming of a harmonious world, it must reckon with a leap that can in no way be explained in terms of present reality.* But in so doing, socialist belief breaks through the bourgeois principle, i.e., the presupposition of a rational world order that is implicit in reality as such. It contains an element of prophetic proclamation, the expectation of a new being. But it formulates this expectation in a way that is completely defined by the bourgeois principle, i.e., as a purely immanent expectation. This it is forced to do because it must resist the attempt of bourgeois society to interpret the prophetic expectation of the end as purely transcendent and thus deprive it of its revolutionary energy. Among the bourgeoisie, transcendent expectation is used as an antirevolutionary ideology. Socialism is compelled to expose this ideology, and, in the process, is forced to the side of pure immanence. In fact, however, its own expectation goes beyond immanence as understood in the bourgeois belief in harmony. The constantly recurring alternation of hope and disappointment, of utopianism and unavoidable compromise, that fills the history of socialism, is the consequence of this inner conflict.

It is understandable that leaders and theoreticians of socialism should seek to avoid this discord by borrowing from the bourgeois belief in progress. In so doing they fall into a *reformism* that abandons the socialist presupposition of disharmony and makes the proletarian movement a purely intrabourgeois affair.[9] It is well known how disastrously this has affected the socialist movement during the last forty years, especially in giving rise to the schism between reformist and revolutionary socialism.

If in this split *Communism* can be said to represent the revolutionary side, one must acknowledge that it has more clearly understood the inevitable shattering of the bourgeois principle of harmony than have the Social Democrats. Communism does not believe in any form of progress on the soil of bourgeois society. It believes in the leap, in the wholly new that is only possible through a complete social revolution. But it holds this belief in the context of a radical this-worldliness; and in this contradiction it consumes itself, leading the proletariat from one disappointment to another. (*Bolshevism* is not a counter example, for in Russia, Communism is also the form in which the principle of rationality has prevailed for the first time on the soil of a social situation reflecting the myth of origin and containing unbroken powers of origin, as was pointed out above. To equate this with the social situation of countries in which the process of rationalization and loss of substance is very far advanced would lead to erroneous conclusions.) The conflict within socialist belief is found among Social Democrats as well as Communists, although it cannot be denied that the intensity of belief is greater in the Communist camp.

It was the basic purpose of *religious socialism* to disclose and to resolve this conflict in socialist belief. Appealing both to Marx and to the prophetic, early Christian end-expectation, it devoted itself to uncovering the element of faith in socialism and making it explicit. Only from this perspective can religious socialism be understood. There is also a socialist movement within the church whose goal is to make the church accessible to the socialist worker and *vice versa*. This task is indeed necessary and is of considerable importance; but it is not fundamentally decisive.

Religious socialism is the attempt to bring into awareness the element of faith at work in socialism, to reveal socialism's inner conflict, and to lead it to a solution that has symbolic power.[10]

2. The Inner Conflict in the Socialist View of Human Nature

The antinomy in the socialist view of human nature constitutes the primary and most important element in the conflict in socialist belief. The bourgeois concept of human nature is developed on the basis of reason. This corresponds to the bourgeois principle, with its desire for a rational formation of reality. Human beings become human by participating in universal reason. *Only* human beings, but also *every* human being, participates in it. The capacity for rationality is the primary characteristic of human being; the other aspects of human nature must be made subject to reason. Things outside of us as well as our own nature within us are in reason's domain. Thereby the level of human being that can be designated as the "center" is lost—a level that is more primordial than the abstractions of subjective reason on the one hand or than an objective drive mechanism on the other. The bourgeois principle obscures this middle level between pure reason and that which is subordinated to it. Consciousness sees only itself and its objects; it does not see being as being, and it does not see the creative and destructive forces by which, in fact, it is determined, and by which it is exalted or torn asunder. *Being, even human being, must be formed by consciousness.* Thus arises the image of humanity as steadily and progressively raising being to the level of consciousness; as gaining an ever clearer self-understanding, as analyzing things and acting on the basis of this illumination (earlier called "enlightenment") in a reasonable, orderly manner, on the heights of the "most advanced consciousness."[11]

In accordance with the tension between liberalism and democracy (in epistemology, between empiricism and rationalism), two tendencies are found in the Enlightenment view of human nature. The *empiricist* tendency, corresponding to liberalism, presupposes that the elements of perception and instinct, by virtue of a demonstrable mechanism, can assume a rational form that in turn enables us to know objects well enough to act toward them in a rational manner. A multiplicity of perceptions are impressed on the *tabula rasa* of the human spirit, and by virtue of a natural harmony an adequate practical knowledge of reality is developed. Likewise the multiplicity of human instincts, in the encounter with nature and with other forms of instinctual life, leads, via the relevant natural laws, to rational behavior within society. Thus is developed a person who fits into the network of social institutions, furthering the welfare of all in the pursuit of the self's own welfare.

The *rationalist* interpretation of human nature, which corresponds to the democratic element of the bourgeois principle, is quite different. It does not share the expectation that a rational knowledge of existence and a rational formation of existence will arise out of the reciprocal interaction of perceptions and instincts. In its view, reason stands beyond such multiplicity. Reason faces it majestically, struggles with it and subjugates it. What for empiricism happens automatically, as it were, is here the result of constant spontaneous activity, a continuous fulfilling of logical and moral demands. The human consciousness itself, as the central authority, creates the world that it knows and rules. This cannot be done immediately or at one stroke. It occurs only through a gradual process, a step by step strengthening of this central authority, i.e., of rational knowledge and will. Education thus plays a decisive role for this line of thought. Since rationality does not develop naturally, education must intervene; the more developed reason must lead the less developed, and bring it to maturity. *All democratic thought is pedagogical thought.* So it was in the Enlightenment; so Lessing gave it classic formulation in his *Education of the Human Race*; and so it is today. However, this belief in a progressive education of the human race contains within itself the liberal belief in harmony, however well the latter may be concealed. It must presuppose that the individual person as well as humanity as a whole is capable of education, that the contents of knowledge are grasped and shaped by the categories of knowledge, and that the instinctual life can be determined by moral categories. The presupposition of this view of human nature is that substance can be apprehended through form, through pure reason, and this presupposition amounts to a belief in harmony.

German socialism combines elements of liberal psychology with strong pedagogical tendencies. Because it combines these two elements in its view of human nature, it falls into conflict with itself. Since it does not share the bourgeois belief in harmony, it can envision humanity as determined by reason in knowledge and action only in the end-time, in the classless society. In the present, as in all past time, i.e., under the rule of disharmony, there are neither laws that lead to a natural harmony, nor the proper conditions for an effective education of the individual and of humanity.[12] These human beings, however, who according to this presupposition are not determined by reason, must somehow bring about a situation in which reason rules. *There is nothing to mediate the leap from unreason to reason. Between reality and expectation lies an abyss.*

Marx distinguishes the "prehistory" of humanity that precedes the emergence of the classless society from the "history" that begins at this point. But we know only prehistory. Human reality encounters us in the form of what he calls prehistory or the history of class struggles. The person who lives in the class struggle is a person whose being is characterized better by Nietzsche's doctrine of the will to power than by Lessing's doctrine of the education of the human race. The question, "How is it possible for the will to power ever to lead to the renunciation of power?" remains unanswered. For this reason, Marxism, in spite of its hostility to utopianism, has never been able to defend itself against the suspicion that it has a hidden faith in utopia. The prophetic expectation of the end is consistent: it looks forward to a miracle of nature that transforms human nature as well as nonhuman nature, and thus it creates the presuppositions for a reign of righteousness. Bourgeois thought believes in a progressive harmony of nature and spirit in human life, i.e., in an ever greater disengagement of humanity from its universal natural foundation and an overcoming of the "will to power." Socialism

shares neither the one presupposition nor the other. When socialist theory asserts that it is the transformation of the social situation that will transform human beings, it avoids the question of
how a transformed social situation is possible without the transformation of human beings. This circle is unbreakable, and has
important practical consequences.

Socialism's adopting of the bourgeois interpretation of human
nature and its consequent exclusion of the "center" from its image
of the human has caused, for example, *the underestimation of the
charismatic personality*, i.e. the person who carries power of
conviction by virtue of his being, his spiritual-vital center, quite
apart from his rational formation or standing. This is the reason
for the lack of symbolically powerful, forceful personages in
German socialism who can create a spirit of *eros* and commitment, as well as for the fact that in a strong reaction against this,
a personality with trivial power of being could become the symbol and *Führer* of revolutionary political romanticism.

From the same source stems the striking *dearth of impressive
symbols* within the socialist movement, be they visual or verbal
symbols. Only recently has this situation begun to change—
without, to be sure, being able to rival the symbol-creating power
of the movements related to the myth of origin.

Even the disillusionment that many socialist theoreticians feel in
the face of what is wrongly called the *petit bourgeois* spirit of the
upper strata of the proletariat finds its explanation here. Nostalgia
for the land, for the family, for a supportive community, etc., can
only be evaluated negatively by the bourgeois *dogmatism*, as we
must call it, of certain intellectuals.[13]

And yet socialism is forced to fight constantly for its view of
human nature, and thus for the bourgeois view, against the
bourgeoisie. For the prebourgeois view of human nature, the
understanding in terms of the origin and of the spiritual and vital
center, serves an ideological function in the situation of class rule,
regardless of the truth it may contain. It serves to justify authoritarian tendencies, to establish bourgeois dominance over the
proletarian movement, and to affirm an eternally uniform essence

of the human, for which certain divinely established orders alone are suitable. In the struggle against this misuse of the prebourgeois view of human nature for the solidifying of class rule, socialism champions the bourgeois principle against the bourgeoisie and against itself as well. This is the conflict in the socialist interpretation of human nature.

3. The Inner Conflict in the Socialist Concept of Society*

The bourgeois concept of society counts on the emergence of a universal, rational will, whether by liberal and natural means or through centralized control and education. Socialism's experience is that in either case, the rule of a particular class prevails, a class that claims to represent the universal rational will, and which creates an appropriate ideology to this effect, but which in fact pursues its own class interest. Belief in social harmony, just like the belief in harmony generally, is shattered on the reality of class. The bourgeoisie has sought to escape this contradiction by *equating bourgeois class interest and the interest of society as a whole*. Over against feudalism, the bourgeoisie to a certain extent was right when, in its struggle against feudal privileges, it believed itself to represent the interest of all individuals without distinction. So long as the split between classes was not visible, the bourgeoisie as "the third estate" could see itself as the final estate, as inclusive of the whole society. It was this belief in the harmony between bourgeois existence and social obligation which gave to the bourgeoisie the sense of certainty that it represented the universal, rational will.

Socialism sets the "fourth estate," the proletariat, against the third estate. Socialism sees in the proletariat the place where that becomes true which in bourgeois society was mere ideology: the harmony of a particular group interest with the interest of society as a whole. The proletarian consciousness is a universal rational

* *Gesellschaftsauffassung.* The author employs the distinction proposed by Tönnies between *Gemeinschaft* and *Gesellschaft,* "community" and "society." Cf. section 5, below.—TRANS.

consciousness. What in the third estate was only an intention—the rule of reason in society—becomes a reality in the fourth estate.

This belief is understandable if one considers the social position of the proletariat. The proletariat requires no ideological cover for a position of power, for it has none. The true structure of society is disclosed in the proletariat, for it is the victim of this structure. Its struggle is the struggle for the whole society, a struggle against the division by which society is destroying itself.

And yet this is all a belief in harmony; it is a bourgeois interpretation of society, but one more radical and more open than the bourgeoisie dared to advocate. But reality contradicts this harmony: for the sake of socialism the proletariat must fight for its class interest over the bourgeois interest. It must use the means of power in order to overcome power in principle. It must deny the state as an instrument of bourgeois class rule, and at the same time must conquer it in order to establish proletarian class rule. The goal of the conquest of the state is the abolition of state, power, and class. *In the present, power is opposed by power so that in the future, power can renounce power.* Socialist belief thus once more shows itself to be a belief in miracles, both in its interpretation of human nature and in its interpretation of society. The bourgeoisie took advantage of its power to effect its own class rule. It broke with the belief in a harmony between the bourgeoisie and society in general that it originally held, although it still maintains it as an ideology. The proletariat, or, more precisely, the militant and power-bearing group of the proletariat, is to give up voluntarily the power that it has won. Here the bourgeois belief in harmony is to prove true, even though it has never done so as regards the bourgeoisie itself. Here power is to overcome itself by reason.

In the relatively short time of its conscious struggle, the proletariat has had experiences that were suited to shake this belief in a harmony between proletarian interest and universal reason. First, a *leadership* emerged out of the proletariat whose interest became quite independent of the interests of the proletariat itself, and which became a sociologically established power group. Numerous tensions have arisen out of this situation, tensions that plainly contradicted the theory of a unified proletarian interest. Secondly, in all European countries, the national interest proved stronger than class interest. The *national power group* has subjected the proletariat to itself. Thirdly, the German proletariat in particular has split into two groups that are quite different, even in their sociological structure, and which to a considerable extent represent contradictory interests. From the standpoint of the radically proletarianized masses that are united under the banner of Communism, the trade-unionist, Social Democratic proletariat has a bourgeois character. In any case, the latter's right to identify its interest with that of the proletariat as a whole and thus also with that of society in general, is contested. The fact of *class division within the proletariat itself* undermines the socialist belief in harmony, just as the fact of class division within the bourgeoisie shattered the bourgeois belief in harmony. Fourthly, German socialism has had occasion to observe that the *proletarianized middle strata*, whose interests, according to the theory, should have led them into the proletarian camp, have in fact been driven by these interests into the sharpest opposition to socialism. In this way, also, belief in the unity of proletarian interest and its equivalence with the universal rational will of reason was shaken.

A direct consequence of this conflict in the socialist interpretation of society is *socialism's uncertain attitude toward the state*. Postwar German history provides continuing evidence of the fateful political consequences of this attitude, as shown in the retreat, with almost no resistance, before the forces of reaction. In the persons of the Social Democratic leadership, a group came to power whose will to power had been destroyed by dogma. So there resulted an uncertain vacillation between the use of power and the renunciation of power. That was particularly noticeable in the *ambivalent attitude toward the armed forces*. On the one hand, they were affirmed as a support of governmental authority, while on the other hand, there was an aversion to them that from the very beginning played right into the hands of

78 THE SOCIALIST DECISION

the reactionaries. The same holds for the filling of *political positions of power*, which was done so timidly and therefore so arbitrarily that the few measures undertaken in this connection stirred up more opposition than a decisive and thorough exercise of political power would have done. All these are consequences of the inner conflict in the socialist interpretation of society. But as soon as socialism attempts to establish and effect a new interpretation of society by breaking through the bourgeois faith in harmony and by acknowledging social disharmony—doing so with the aid of the powers of origin—it falls into the difficulty that is inherent in the proletarian situation: the idea of power, with all its consequences for the conception of the state, for both domestic and foreign policy, has long since been co-opted by bourgeois society for the cementing of its class rule. The bourgeoisie restricts its principle as narrowly as possible as soon as it sees possibilities for securing its position with the help of pre-bourgeois forces and ideologies. Socialism therefore stands in necessary contradiction to all ideologies of power. It must fight on its own in favor of the bourgeois principle against the bourgeoisie, not in order to preserve it but in order to shatter it.

The attitude of socialism toward the constitution of the state also suffers particularly under these difficulties. With a decisiveness shown on hardly any other issue, German socialism has drawn the consequences of the bourgeois principle for this question. It has made democracy the constitutive principle for the construction of society, in all groups, small and large, and indeed a democracy in which every remnant of a tie to the origin has disappeared by virtue of the abstract technique of elections. The bond between the electorate and those elected has been cut. The act of electing has become a purely mechanical procedure, the formation of a majority a problem of mathematics. It is fateful that with this radicalization of the bourgeois principle, socialism has politically discredited not only democracy, but, to a large extent, also itself. It was seduced into adopting this extreme position by its old struggle against the bourgeois and feudal restraints that, in the prewar period, hampered democracy and enhanced class rule.[14] Here, too, we see the inner conflict into which socialism has been driven by the alliance of the bourgeoisie and feudalism in building the class society.

4. The Inner Conflict in the Socialist Idea of Culture

The socialist idea of culture and community directly follows from the socialist interpretation of human nature and of society. The socialist idea of culture is expressed in socialism's attitude toward religion, science, education, and intellectual life and work. In all of these areas, the inner conflict of socialism becomes visible, and in all of them it has definite practical consequences. In the first period of the socialist movement, it was possible to put aside these questions. Indeed, this was required by the sort of struggle being waged. Nevertheless, these questions took on all the greater importance when socialism changed from a movement exclusively oriented toward struggle into a force participating in the determination of cultural policy. The struggle for socialism has long since become as much a struggle for the socialist idea of culture as for the socialist idea of economics. It is not admissible to put aside these questions until the "day after the successful revolution." For the success of the revolution depends on the inspiring power of an expectation in which all aspects of human existence find a new fulfillment; and the success of the revolution requires persons whose being and consciousness is formed through their anticipation of the coming fulfillment.

The religious foundation of socialism—socialist belief and its roots in human existence—have been shown. *Socialism is religious if religion means living out of the roots of human being.* But this concept of religion, which especially religious socialism presents as the only legitimate one, is very different from the concept of religion assumed in socialism's programmatic statements. When the Erfurt Program* declared religion to be a private matter, it was thinking of a separate sphere of human thought and action existing alongside numerous other spheres. In

---

* Manifesto adopted by the German Social Democrats at the party congress of 1891.—TRANS.

contrast, if we speak of socialist belief, we do not refer to religion as a separate sphere, but as the power supporting and determining all spheres.

In socialist cultural policy, the question does not concern this second, deeper concept of religion, but rather the first-mentioned concept, that of a separate phenomenon alongside others. In making the statement that religion is a private matter, socialism places itself on the side of the *liberal, bourgeois idea of tolerance*. It opposes the churches' claims to political power, it opposes state churches and the political misuse of religion. To make religion a private matter means to exclude it from the arena of political struggles, and to turn it over to the individual or to a free association of individuals. As in all other respects, so here, too, socialism draws the consequences of the bourgeois principle. The German situation gave it many opportunities to do so. Hegel's effort to establish a philosophical foundation for positive Christianity, especially his ambiguous Christology, was the most important expression of the alliance of the bourgeoisie and feudalism. Very soon after the collapse of Hegel's system, the feudal and orthodox element which Hegel had united with the bourgeois, liberal element, gained the upper hand. The Enlightenment, i.e., the intellectual struggle of the revolutionary bourgeoisie, was forgotten or discredited. An orthodox state church gained dominance; with its help a bourgeois feudal state made up of reactionaries gave itself a basis and a blessing. This was German socialism's hour of birth. It was inevitable that it should ally itself with bourgeois radicalism and fight not only against the state religion that had come to power, but also against the idealistic combination of Enlightenment and orthodoxy. Socialism took over bourgeois radicalism's offensive weapons, above all the materialistic interpretation of human nature as represented by Feuerbach in his opposition to Hegel. Since that time, and on the basis of this situation of conflict (which still has its effects today), the socialist movement has stood on the side of materialism against idealism, of liberalism against orthodoxy, and of atheism rather than any kind of authoritarian religion. So it was thrust into the sharpest opposition to the churches, and it has maintained this opposition down to the present, while the liberal bourgeoisie, after its victorious penetration of state and society, made peace with the church and with dogma. Rejecting its own authentic history, it abandoned theological liberalism.[15] *Socialism is the only group to uphold the bourgeois principle with reference to the church and religion.* This situation, however, conflicts with the spirit of the socialist movement. Socialist belief, as the basis of socialist thought and action, finds expression in all socialistic activity. Usually it is not thrust into the foreground and raised to an explicit level; frequently the proletariat and its leadership know little of it and its significance; but it is there, and it is nourished by both roots of human being—the bond to the origin and the expectation of the new. And in both respects, socialist belief transcends the bourgeois principle.

The attitude of socialism toward religion could never have been as negative as it has become, if socialism had not thought that it had a substitute for religion at its disposal, namely, *science*, and indeed science in the sense of bourgeois positivism. Here, too, it is necessary to understand the attitude of socialism in terms of the period in which it originated. The triumph of the scientific method (specifically that of the natural sciences) that characterized the seventeenth and eighteenth centuries was brought to a standstill on the threshold of the nineteenth century by the romantic reaction. The resurgence of prebourgeois forces during those years threatened the rational knowledge and mastery of the world. Mythical forms which had been repressed from consciousness for two centuries reemerged and discredited rational science. To be sure, this was only a brief interlude. Natural science freed itself very quickly, and very passionately, from the chains of the new *mythos*. What was at stake was the being or nonbeing of the bourgeoisie, and here it proved its ascendant, victorious power. It was otherwise in the humanities and the social sciences; with these, the bourgeoisie was less concerned. Indeed, it had an interest in preventing the exposure of the class situation by a scientific analysis of capitalism.[16] Marx accomplished in his social teaching what the bourgeoisie did in natural science. He broke the spell of the romantic ideologies. So far as the natural sciences were concerned, socialism joined the bourgeoisie in its battle against the prebourgeois powers; so far as the social sciences were concerned, it fought simultaneously against both the bourgeoisie and the prebourgeois powers. Thus it is understandable that the scientific study of nature and society was regarded by socialism as its own strongest weapon. Furthermore, it was through socialism that the proletariat for the first time was brought into contact with science and that it was given a self-consciousness in the form of scientific concepts. Socialism's unconditional *faith in science,* and especially the reverence for science shown by the proletarian masses, can be understood in terms of these circumstances surrounding its origin.

Socialism did not notice that the way in which the proletariat revered science lacked all the characteristics of a genuinely scientific attitude, and had, rather, all the characteristics of religious belief. It was not noticed that the basic scientific concepts had long since become symbols and dogma in the proletarian consciousness. It was overlooked that in the proletarian belief in science two elements were combined in a contradictory manner: *socialist belief and scientific method.*

But even if socialism had been conscious of this, its attitude toward science would still have been basically the same. Socialism had to defend the bourgeois principle of rational analysis against a bourgeoisie that was behaving in a mystical and irrational way in order to ward off the revolutionary consequences of a thoroughgoing analysis of society, in order to legitimate itself by means of a bourgeois historical legend and to fog over the abyss that divided the classes. Against these feudal-bourgeois "syntheses," socialism must always press for radical analysis. It must expose the bourgeois ideology with the aid of the bourgeois idea of science. It must press for the strictest empiricism and the most rigorous methodology, and must espouse critical thought over against mystical intuition. But in so doing, socialism, in this respect also, comes into conflict with itself. For the power from which its vision of human fulfillment and of a just society is derived is not the power of analysis. It is the power of undivided being that presses toward a new fulfillment beyond the disunity into which it has fallen. A conflict of great depth and with serious consequences follows from this situation.

Socialism's attitude toward religion and science finds its practical consequences in *education*. The significance of pedagogy for bourgeois democratic thought has already been shown. Socialism grasped its importance and put itself politically in the service of antiecclesiastical and antiauthoritarian education. In this, too, it acted as the heir of the bourgeoisie and radicalized the bourgeois principle. It took up the demand for a general education for every individual, leading toward rationality and maturity, and sought to effectuate it over against all monopolies of education.[17] The very undemocratic class character of bourgeois education (not in principle, but in actuality) was challenged in the name of the idea of an "education of the human race." The difficulty begins the moment one asks about the content of universal human maturity and rationality. Socialism knows through its insight into the class situation and class ideology that the content of these concepts varies greatly according to the class situation. It knows that the belief of the Enlightenment in a *universal human reason* and its classical expression in antiquity was in the first instance a polemical weapon of the bourgeoisie against feudalism, and then became a defensive weapon against the proletariat, i.e., mere ideology. Only by contradicting itself could socialism have maintained a belief in universal reason after having recognized the splits in human reason, and its conditioning by special interests and its dependence on social groups, long before bourgeois relativism had gained these insights. But it was equally impossible for socialism to affirm the educational goals of the prebourgeois, confessional, and other groups bound to the origin. It had to represent the *secular school* over against the churches, but since a "secularism" with a clear and simple meaning does not exist (for bourgeois and socialist "secularism" contradict one another), it would have had to transform the secular school, as far as possible, into a socialist school. It would have had to try to make socialist belief the basis of its pedagogy. But it shied away from this, partly because socialist belief had not yet become a matter of conscious awareness, partly because it feared that this would promote the confessionalization of the schools, and partly because of its faith in science. Here, again is a conflict whose concrete expression is the concept of the secular school, for which it must struggle and yet which it cannot believe in.

The socialist concept of education implies the socialist position on questions of *cultural and intellectual life*. This position also contains an antinomy. The bourgeois concept of human nature leads to an ideal of intellectual expression and human formation that, despite individual differences, is universally human and eternally valid. Its realization is achieved to a greater or lesser degree according to the spiritual and personal power of particular individuals or peoples. The great creations of culture in which human being comes to purest expression provide a norm for all cultural achievements, and are the vehicles of all education. In them an overarching reason is expressed, individually and yet universally, temporally and yet with eternal validity. *Socialism stands in contradiction to this concept, which is humanist in the classic sense of that term.* It attacks the idea of an overarching reason, for it knows the inseparable connection of every intellectual creation with the limited human situation out of which it arises. It knows an intellect that is bound to class, an intellect in which a particular human situation of struggle, of domination, or of repression comes to self-consciousness. Intellect, so understood, is not universally human, but is the expression of a particular social being; and education, so understood, is not the transmission of universal cultural values, but a process of being shaped in a particular social situation—a situation of struggle—by the creations in which these particular human possibilities are expressed or have in the past been expressed.

This basic notion creates a difficult problem for socialism. The proletarian situation, as the utmost degree of objectification and loss of the powers of origin, makes an independent socialist cultural productivity almost impossible. Very few instances of such are extant, and where this has been explicitly taken as an aim, as in the movement that adopted the ridiculous name *Proletkultur,*°

° An obscure German movement probably modelled after the *Proletarskaja Kultura* ("Proletarian Culture") movement in the Soviet Union, which flourished especially in the years immediately following the Bolshevik Revolution of 1917.—TRANS.

something resulted quite different from genuine creations of the proletarian spirit. So the energies of socialism in the sphere of culture were expended in defending the bourgeois, humanistic cultural ideal against the cultural reactionaries, and in making that ideal a basis for popular education. As a result of its alliance with prebourgeois powers, the bourgeoisie itself had undermined the humanist ideal of culture, and had adapted its cultural activity to the new situation. It attached full participation in these cultural achievements to particular economic presuppositions; they had become a class privilege. The proletariat received only the scraps left over from the humanist ideal, without depth, without enthusiasm, and without a real inner relation to its own situation. Thus socialism was forced to bring bourgeois culture to the proletariat, thereby, however, entering into contradiction with its own insight regarding the inseparable connection between social situation and cultural life, between being and an authentic formation of being. *The fate of the people's high school movement* [*Volkshochschulbewegung*] *and of all of socialism's efforts in the sphere of culture has its roots, for good and ill, in this conflict, the conflict in the socialist concept of culture.*

5. *The Inner Conflict in the Socialist Idea of Community**

As for nature, so too for the human community, the bourgeois principle implies a process of resolving something into its constituent elements, i.e., into individuals—in the expectation, to be sure, that the natural laws of harmony will bring about a new community on a higher level than that of communities bound to the origin.

The so-called "atomization" of the life of the community by liberalism means, first of all, an acknowledgment of the rights of the individual in the sense of the prophetic and humanistic premise. It means the abrogation of the bonds of origin that oppress and crush the individual. The bourgeois doctrine of natural law not only broke down the forms of political domination; it also

---

* *Gemeinschaftsidee.* See note on p. 75 above.—TRANS.

weakened and partly dissolved all remaining communal bonds of a prebourgeois sort. The ties to the land were cut by the right to choose one's own place of residence, the bonds to social rank by the abrogation of privileges, bonds to one's ethnic group and family through the abrogation of ancestral rights, bonds to race and region through the emergence of the centralized national state. The emancipation of the individual from all prior conditions, from the power of origin that supported him, was carried through as far as the needs of bourgeois society dictated. But only just this far. The alliance with prebourgeois strata, the use of the remnants of patriarchalism for grounding and strengthening the rule of capital, restricted the operation of the bourgeois principle. And nationalism almost completely eclipsed the idea of world citizenship which liberalism had inspired. Women and children were firmly held in patriarchal dependency, the rural proletariat was denied basic rights, and in relations between the sexes, bourgeois legalism and feudal traditions entered into an alliance that was just as effective as it was devoid of inner truth.[18]

In this situation, the proletariat was forced by virtue of its own existence to radicalize the bourgeois principle. In so doing, it went hand in hand with the remnants of the revolutionary bourgeoisie. The industrial proletariat is the place, by reason of its structure, in which the dissolution of all communal bonds has been most completely effected. The individual as an independent marketer of his own power of labor is cast back entirely upon himself. Women and children are in the same situation as men; basically, the family is dissolved. The concept of rank or station cannot be applied to the proletariat; it is not a rank but a class. Attachments to one's place of work or working group have no binding power; they are dissolved as soon as the market demands a change. Regarding the relation of the sexes, neither feudal nor bourgeois-feudal models have any symbolic power. Local, regional, and national communities have basically no reality for proletarian existence. The consciousness of the proletariat corresponds to its being. The freeing of the individual from bonds of origin that have become meaningless is demanded with a relentless consistency. Ancestral relationships between "ruler and retainer," between master and apprentice, between husband and wife, between parents and children are attacked politically and intellectually. Traditions—for example, those of the church—are, so far as they are not voluntarily abolished, despised as unprogressive. *Every form of tradition or bond is seen, on the soil of capitalism, as a means of class rule.*

Thereby, however, the inner conflict of the socialist idea of community is revealed. Socialism, supported by the proletariat and its fate, serves as the executor of all the dissolving powers of the bourgeois principle. But it at the same time is the attack upon the bourgeois principle. It must therefore propose a form of community in contrast to that which is disintegrating. It cannot believe that through the freeing of all individuals, harmony will follow as by a natural law. In reality, what follows is the opposition of classes that characterizes and divides all communities. Socialism must therefore fall back upon powers of origin in order to make community possible. But as soon as it does this, it finds itself aligned with the feudal ideology whose intent is to buttress its own class rule by pretending to offer a form of community based on the powers of origin.

This is especially true for the *attitude of socialism toward the idea of the nation.* In accordance with the bourgeois principle, socialism breaks through national limitations and advocates an international ideal of humanity. In the last analysis, it must place humankind above the nation, and draw from this its conclusions regarding international law. At the same time, however socialism is dependent for its own realization on national powers of origin. It has learned that the concrete community of place, race, and culture, is, in spite of the opposition of classes, stronger than the abstract identity of its destiny to that of the proletariat in other countries. It understands that it must actualize itself nationally if it is to actualize itself at all. The bourgeois belief in harmony is shattered for socialism on this point also. The dissolution of the bonds of origin does not lead at all to a united humanity, but rather to an economic struggle among the capitalistic nations and to imperialistic war. Socialism is thus thrown back upon the nation as a power of origin which it, too, cannot avoid. *The idea of* *the nation, however, had proven to be the most important instrument of domination in the hands of capital.* Socialism thus falls into the conflict of having to be internationalistic over against national imperialism, and on the other hand, nationalistic over against the ideology of international citizenship. It is in view of this conflict that one can understand, for example, the fact that although it put the needs of the nation first in the revolution and the civil war, and then in the struggle for domination of the Ruhr[*] and in the problem of inflation, even to the point of destroying itself as a party, social democracy was charged with being unpatriotic by the so-called "national movement," which at no time had to practice such self-denial for the nation. This is not simply demagogy[19]; it has its basis precisely in this conflict, which forces socialism to carry through the bourgeois principle against itself, while at the same time forcing it to deny this principle in the name of concrete communal forces.

With respect to other *forms of community*, socialism has a similar attitude as it does towards the nation. Socialism cannot advocate as its own the disintegrating consequences of the bourgeois principle with respect to the family, social rank, ties to the soil and to particular localities. And yet it must constantly do so. It cannot avoid this conflict with the help of the concept of *solidarity*. Solidarity refers in the first instance to a purposive, fighting community, and thus is dependent on the existence of an opponent. If it is no more than this, it breaks asunder as soon as the enemy is eliminated, or it is dissolved in inner contradictions. The history of the labor movement is full of examples of this. But if solidarity is understood as the expression of a unity that also exists apart from a common struggle and a common enemy, then it rests on some form of origin, on *eros* and destiny, and is not grounded in reason. The question then arises "How is such unity possible on the grounds of a disintegrating proletarian situation?" The answer points back to the powers of origin: family, nation, religion, etc. But these concepts have become means of struggle

[*] A reference to the struggle between France and Germany from 1919 to 1925 for the coal and heavy industry near the conjunction of the Ruhr and Rhine rivers.—TRANS.

in the hands of capitalistic domination, and cannot simply be used without any further ado. Thus every way out appears to be cut off, in this respect as with the other antinomies of socialism.

6. *The Inner Conflict in the Socialist Idea of Economics*

The fullest expression of the bourgeois belief in harmony is the liberal idea of economics. Here the notion of *laissez faire* with regard to all forces of production, of unrestrained competition, has its true home. *The laws of the market are the rational basis of the belief in harmony.* They demonstrate how, out of conflict, harmony must result, i.e., the greatest possible advantage for all.

On no point did the socialist opposition take so firm and unambiguous a stand as here. The actual result of liberal economics was class rule and imperialistic war, the crisis of the proletarian masses and their utter insecurity. It is all the more remarkable that even here, socialism had to enter into the bourgeois legacy. When hindrances and disorders in the market mechanism arose from the alliance of the bourgeoisie and feudalism, socialism had to range itself on the side of liberalism. *It had to accept the claim that the best possible provision for the greatest number is guaranteed by an economy that works rationally.* It had to seek to exclude the irrational elements that had been inserted into the economic process by groups bound to the myth of origin such as large landholders, artisans, and the peasantry. Above all it had to reject the disturbance of the market laws that flowed from nationalism. It had to range itself on the side of free trade against import duties, on the side of the independent entrepreneur against governmental protectionism. It had to reject the idea of a national autarky (an idea that is presently quite influential), with its agrarian political background. Here, again, the proletarian situation forces socialism to radicalize the liberal principle of economics, and to oppose the attempt to feudalize, for example, heavy industry. Even though at the moment the security of one economic group, and thereby also that of the proletariat belonging to it, may be attained by limiting the liberal principle, in the long run it creates a worsening of economic conditions generally, and soon also reacts back upon the proletarian groups that had been favored. The temporary improvement of market conditions for a particular domestic group, for example, cannot delude the proletariat, even if it profits from it, since it has to pay for its advantage in terms of an increase in the price of goods in its own country, and, in the long run, by a worsening of sales because of retaliatory measures. Thus everything appears to drive the proletariat toward an affirmation of the free market. But at the same time, everything speaks against it. The proletariat experiences the destruction of the liberal principle in the frightful irrationality of the economic crisis.[20] It knows from experience that the liberal method in economics leads to periods of terrible pauperization, and furthermore that even under the most favorable of market conditions, the share of the proletariat in the goods produced is extremely modest in comparison to the share of the opposing class. It experiences the class struggle as a reality that is inseparably bound up with the free enterprise economy, a reality that annuls its claim to be the most rational economic scheme. Thus the antiliberal economic premise of socialism arises: the demand that free disposition over the means of production be abolished and that the crisis-creating state of unrestrained competition be replaced by centralized planning. Socialism places itself on the side of the antiliberal position in economics: central control instead of *laissez faire*, leadership from above instead of faith in harmony from below. In this way socialism shifts from the liberal to the democratic aspect of the bourgeois principle. *Rationality in economics is not to be abrogated but is to be placed into the hands of human beings.* They are to accomplish what nature could not: the best possible supply of economic goods for all.

But this raises the question, "Who is the agent that shall accomplish what the natural laws of economics could not accomplish?" The only kind of agent that would be capable of doing this would be one that was united with pure reason, both in theoretical superiority and in thoroughness of practical expertise. In the place of nature, which has disappointed, there enters humanity, which shall not disappoint. But why not? Here is the element of belief in harmony which democracy and liberalism have in common. It is a belief in the possibility of harmony between a centralized planning mind and the scattered manifold of economic realities. *A pure economic consciousness is postulated that provides the laws of harmony which are vainly sought in nature.*

It remains unclear, however, where this pure consciousness is supposed to come from, of which power group one can presuppose that its own interests at the same time represent pure economic reason. If the bourgeois belief in harmony is given up—and that is what socialism has done—then one cannot expect to find any such groups. Even the proletariat itself has many conflicting interests. Thus a return to the powers of origin seems unavoidable. It appears as if socialism must work for an economic leadership that is carried out through the cooperation and compromise of different power groups. And yet it cannot do this, since these groups, in a class society, are the instrumentalities of class rule, and therefore cannot be addressed as representatives of a comprehensive economic reason. Thus the deep inner conflict of socialism shows itself once again, and in it, the conflict of the proletarian situation.

Conclusion: Socialist Praxis

Our presentation of the inner conflict of socialism in all its dimensions has not been derived abstractly and deductively, but from the tensions in actual socialist thought and action. We intentionally did not concern ourselves expressly with Marxism. Insofar as Marxism is coextensive with the socialist understanding of reality, all that has been said concerning the inner conflict of socialism is valid for it as well. Insofar as Marxism differs from the typical socialist consciousness, it requires special treatment.

The opposition between socialism and Communism, likewise, plays no role in the inner conflict of the proletarian situation or of the socialist movement. Both groups have the same problematic. *Communism does not escape the conflict any more than socialism does.* Communism's more radical praxis, imbued with a stronger political passion, indeed reveals the inner conflict even more

clearly. One can put both parties—not entirely, but to a considerable extent—on both sides of the antinomy. Socialism remains
closer to the liberal-democratic foundation which the bourgeoisie
and socialism have in common. Communism is more ready to
renounce this foundation in the present, because it has a stronger
faith in its miraculous advent in the future. It can ally itself more
easily therefore with certain tendencies in revolutionary romanticism. But this contrast is not an exclusive one, for Social Democracy is also ready, under certain circumstances, to sacrifice the
liberal element, while Communism can never give unqualified
support to the reestablishment of the powers of origin.

The praxis of both parties gives evidence of the inner conflict in
tactics and strategy. They must, at all events, defend the bourgeois principle against the reactionary forces of political romanticism; even the communists have understood this vis-à-vis National Socialism. *They must agree to nonsocialistic measures in
order to preserve the basis for the socialist struggle.* The policy of
the German Social Democrats after the war was altogether determined by this necessity. But they often quite forgot that support
of the bourgeois principle by socialism still does not constitute a
socialist achievement. They forgot that the bourgeoisie is ready to
betray socialism whenever it can enter into an alliance with prebourgeois powers, even if it owes its victory over these powers
wholly to socialism. Thus the German Social Democratic party
was disappointed to find that the bourgeoisie showed gratitude
neither for its sacrifices on behalf of the nation nor for its resolute
defense of the bourgeois principle.

Through these events, the Social Democratic party has been
pressed to the side of Communism, insofar as the latter stands
opposed to the united bourgeois-feudal front. Thereby it has won
the freedom to present demands that derive exclusively from the
socialist principle; but the possibility of effecting any such demands is lost, a situation in which Communism found itself ever
since its inception. The Social Democrats must tolerate for the
time being the reactionary measures that advanced capitalism
employs to maintain its bourgeois-feudal rule.[21] In laying down
its democratic responsibility, the Social Democrats lay down a

difficult burden, but now it must witness how the burden of reaction is laid on the whole nation, and especially on the proletariat. To be sure, democracy did not prove to be in any way a means to overcome class rule, but it could at least impede the consolidation of this rule in feudal form. Therefore the struggle of Social Democracy for democratic structures was grounded in the proletarian situation itself; this is what justified the struggle and made it necessary. But it also showed how the political praxis of socialism is determined by the same conflict which pervades all aspects of socialism. This conflict can be overcome only through a new understanding and application of the socialist principle.

PART THREE:

THE PRINCIPLE OF

SOCIALISM AND THE

SOLUTION OF ITS

INNER CONFLICT

CHAPTER 5

The Socialist Principle and Its Roots

1. The Powers of Origin in the Proletarian Movement

The internal conflict of socialism is rooted in the internal conflict of the proletarian situation. A resolution of this conflict is possible, therefore, only if there is a resolution of the conflict in the proletarian situation itself. Only if forces are visible in the proletariat that transcend the proletarian situation will it be possible to resolve the antinomy of socialism. A theoretical analysis of the conflict resolved by a theoretical synthesis with no corresponding movement in reality would be no solution. Therefore we must ask whether, and to what extent, the proletariat is involved in a movement that can be regarded as the solution of the internal conflict of the proletarian situation. The possibility of giving a positive answer to this question is the presupposition for a resolution of the conflict in its various aspects, and thereby for a fresh realization of socialism.

The conflict of the proletarian situation is rooted in the fact that, on the one hand, the proletariat must draw the consequences of the bourgeois principle, while, on the other hand, it stands in opposition to the bourgeois principle. It must, therefore, overcome the bourgeois principle by means of the bourgeois principle! This is an inescapable conflict, because proletarian existence is the consistent expression of the bourgeois principle. Objectification, depersonalization, and separation from the origin find undisguised expression in the proletariat. From this it would seem to follow that the proletariat cannot react against the bourgeois spirit except in a bourgeois spirit, and thus is irretrievably captive to this spirit.

But this consequence does not follow in reality. If it did, the reaction that ensues in the class struggle would be incomprehensible. Something that has become merely a thing no longer resists its being made into a thing. The reaction of the proletarian, in contrast, is the reaction of a real human being: not the being posited in a rational system, but a being that continues to be related to the origin, deriving from the origin the power to protect itself from being totally cut off from the roots of its being. There is in fact no object either in nature itself or among the purest products of technology that is merely a thing, and that does not retain some final element of inner power with which it resists total absorption into the technical system. It is all the more true that no human being will let himself or herself be utterly deprived of the power of self-determination. *That which reacts in the proletarian is the same as that which political romanticism makes the sole principle of human nature and of society—the origin.* Here is the point where they stand together in opposition to the bourgeois principle. They differ only in that, presupposing this relation to the origin, political romanticism seeks to reject the bourgeois principle, while socialism seeks to incorporate it. In this light we can understand that in spite of their common point of departure, namely, the elevation of humanity as opposed to the dehumanizing bourgeois principle, political romanticism attacks socialism so forcefully. The bourgeoisie from its inception has guarded itself, both psychologically and socially, against a complete severance of its connection with the origin. It has never consistently carried through its own principle. The proletariat, by contrast, was forced into such consistency by its situation. Under the pressure of its situation, the proletariat concealed from itself and from its opponents the point of departure of its own movement, namely, the struggle for humanity. Above all, the socialist theoreticians never understood what the bourgeois grasped instinctively, i.e. that a rational, analytical principle can never become the basis for individual or social life. It can never be more than a corrective and a critical norm. The difficulty of socialist theory lay in the fact that on the one hand it spoke of a total objectification of the proletariat; i.e., it equated the economic situation of the proletariat, in which wage workers sell their labor, with their human situation as a whole. On the other hand, the very proletarian who had become merely a thing was hailed as the vanguard and bearer of a new social order. These two notions cannot be reconciled. The error lies in the first of them. The economic situation is not a sufficient basis for interpreting the human situation. On the contrary, the element of the human in the proletarian reacts against the economic situation. *There remains an element of proletarian being which has not been reduced to the status of a thing, and from this element there emerges the struggle against the bourgeois principle.* The proletarian movement is the reaction of the element of the human in the proletarian against the threat of total human objectification because of economic objectification.

Socialist theoreticians, in their justifiable interest in depicting the proletarian situation in the full range of its negativity, have in many ways rendered poor service to the proletariat. They have supplied their opponents with an arsenal of weapons for maintaining that the proletariat has neither the power to lead a revolutionary struggle nor the inner strength to serve as the basis for a new society.[1] Such assertions, however, falsify the reality of proletarian existence as it is represented in the proletarian movement. *The proletarian movement means much more than simply the political struggle for socialism.* Related to this struggle, yet not identical with it, are such groups as the labor movement, producers' and consumers' cooperatives, and various organizations for religious, intellectual, and educational purposes. Significant too are the differentiations within the proletariat—the various competing or cooperating power groups and workers' associations—as well as the configuration of relationships between the sexes and between the generations. There are various spiritual movements that seek to express positions on questions concerning work, recreation, love, destiny, and death. There is also still a significant legacy of regional and national traditions,

even among those completely reduced to proletarian status.
There are all the tendencies that are characterized by the dubious
term *petit bourgeois*, which are really nothing other than expressions of a longing for the supportive powers of origin. We must
mention also the various communities and sects of a political or
religious kind, the proletarian youth movement, and the ways in
which the combative instinct finds expression in military organization and maneuvers. Important also is the proletariat's attitude
toward the body, toward living things, and toward the land, and
above all, proletarian heroism and readiness to sacrifice. All of
these elements, to which a considerable number of others could
be added, are, to be sure, colored by the class structure and by a
socialist consciousness. But they also have a larger significance.
They are not restricted to specific social classes. They belong
quite generally to the history of humanity as such. The proletariat
has these qualities too, and through them it is related to the other
groups. The primordial elements of human existence are active
among the proletariat; and only because this is the case can there
be a proletariat and a socialism that constitutes a struggle for
humanity, a defense against the destruction of the human by the
bourgeois principle.

*The proletariat and the bond of origin, therefore, are not in
contradiction.* Proletarian being and the proletarian movement
are based on the powers of origin, though in a form that is re-
fracted through the bourgeois principle. Out of this situation the
socialist principle emerges, a principle that can be understood
and grasped afresh only when one considers the two roots of
political thought.

2. The Elements of the Socialist Principle

The elements from which the socialist principle is formed derive from the roots of political thought and their concrete historical expression in political romanticism and in bourgeois society;
from the shattering of the bourgeois principle in the class struggle; and from the inner conflict in socialism. *Socialism is
grounded in the interaction of three elements: the power of the*

origin, the shattering of the belief in harmony, and an emphasis on the demand. The socialist principle contains a yes to the presupposition of political romanticism (the power of origin) and a yes to the presupposition of the bourgeois principle (the breaking of the bond of origin by an unconditional demand), together with a no to the metaphysical core of the bourgeois principle (the belief in harmony). These three elements are interrelated in such a manner that when the presupposition of the bourgeois principle is affirmed, the bond of origin in the sense of political romanticism is broken, and when the bourgeois belief in harmony is rejected, room is made for the powers of origin. The three elements are to be combined in the concept of "expectation," which thereby becomes not just a concept in the narrow sense but a symbol. *Socialism lifts up the symbol of expectation against the myth of origin and against the belief in harmony. It has elements of both, but it transcends both.* Our discussion of the socialist principle and the power it contains, therefore, will rely on the symbol of expectation.

By combining the three elements of the socialist principle in the symbol of expectation, the socialist movement is brought into an explicit relationship with the prophetic tradition. For in the prophets, i.e. in the historical movement in which the second root of human existence was grasped in a radical manner, these three elements likewise are united: the bond of origin, expressed in the form of patriarchal religion; the breaking of the bond of origin by the unconditional demand; and the fulfillment of the origin not in a present interpreted in terms of harmony, but in a promised future. This means that *the socialist principle, so far as its substance is concerned, is prophetic.* Socialism is a prophetic movement, but it exists in a context in which the myth of origin has been broken and the bourgeois principle has become dominant. *Socialism is prophetism on the soil of an autonomous, self-sufficient world.* This perspective is confirmed by the historical fact that socialism is dependent on the revolutionary Christian sects, which themselves derive from the prophetic element in primitive Christianity. No one really understands socialism who ignores its prophetic character. The fact that it can be ignored is attributable to the autonomous nature of socialist forms of life and thought. That it must not be ignored is indicated by any in-depth analysis of these forms, and above all, by a clear grasp of the socialist principle.

The socialist principle can be comprehended in the symbol of expectation. We shall interpret its separate elements, in their specific meaning and in their interrelationships, in terms of this symbol, and these elements, in turn, will give character and substance to the symbol.

Whatever else may be suggested by the word *expectation*, the contrast is clear between this concept, on the one hand, and the myth of origin and political romanticism, on the other hand. Expectation is tension with a forward aim. Expectation directs itself towards what is not now, but shall be, towards something unconditionally new that has never been but is in the making. The fulfillment of being is not to be found in the unfolding of the origin between birth and death. The ambiguity of the origin makes this impossible. There are no eternal laws that regulate all social existence, laws such as political romanticism would use to justify itself theologically. Humanity is a new possibility vis-à-vis nature. In history, this new possibility is realized. But because it is realized in *history*, no present time can be affirmed as the fulfillment of this possibility. History drives forward from every present into the future. History is tension towards that which is to come; concretely, towards the new order of things. The prophet awaits it; socialism strains towards it, regardless of how this straining may be expressed rationally. History, in each of its moments, points beyond itself. Only in this way can history be seen as history, as tension towards the unconditionally new.

Since prophetic expectation is a basic component of the Christian faith, it was not easy for political romanticism to set it aside completely. Religiously oriented conservative romanticism, in particular, runs into difficulties whenever it tries to unite its principle with Christianity. It is tripped up by expectation, the basic attitude of primitive Christianity. Therefore it was forced to try altering the prophetic element without getting rid of it completely. This was done, as it has been done from time immemorial, by attempting *to refer humanity's final expectation to the destiny of the individual soul,* and to sever it from historical destiny, the transformation of the world.[2] The individual expects his end and his fulfillment as a new creature immediately. The movement of history as a whole is not seriously included in this expectation. History again becomes a circle of circles in which human suffering and divine grace contend with one another, but nothing fundamentally new happens. Therefore, one concludes, every expectation that seeks to restructure reality must lead to disappointment. Both in the life of the individual and in political life, irrational powers hold sway. One must subject oneself to them, for they are derived from the irrational depths of the divine itself. One dare not revolt against such powers and "authorities," regardless of how destructive they may be.[3] The new lies beyond history; in history itself, no change is possible.

In contrast to this theological justification of political romanticism, socialism places itself decisively on the side of expectation. It too knows the frustrations of history. It too does not expect human existence and historical reality to be transformed miraculously. It reckons with the possibility of chaos and barbarism in either the immediate or the distant future. Nevertheless, it does not give up expectation as a basic human attitude, any more than the prophets did, despite their deep disappointments. *Prophecy is not divination; it is not a way to calculate or predict coming events.* The fulfillment of a prediction does not confirm the prophetic function, nor does the lack of such a fulfillment invalidate it. The prophetic attitude presupposes only that history as such, in each moment, is oriented toward the new, toward that which is demanded and promised. Expectation is not a subjective attitude. It is grounded in the movement of events themselves. It *is,* so to speak, this movement—though this must not be objectified and turned into the utopian expectation of a coming age of fulfillment. *Fulfillment is not a merely empirical concept.* If it is so interpreted, utopianism necessarily results, and with it that disappointment on which all objective final expectations come to ruin. But it would be equally wrong to rest in an objective fixation on the origin, as per the slogan so beloved of political romanticism: "There is nothing new under the sun." Expectation is a going forward. As such, it overcomes an objectified bond of origin ("Everything remains the same") as well as an objectified final expectation ("Someday everything will become new"). It is a nonobjectified expectation ("The new breaks into the old"). Socialism has a prophetic character because it assumes this posture; but it is threatened constantly, as is the prophetic attitude in all ages, with the possibility of falling into either the one or the other kind of objectification. The socialist movement evidences equally clearly both the basic prophetic attitude and the chronic tendency to relapse into either resignation or utopianism.

3. Expectation and Action

Insofar as expectation is directed toward the new, it contains two factors that stand in a peculiar and momentous tension. That which is expected is that which will come to pass, and, insofar as it *will* come, it is not dependent on human activity. But that which is expected is that which *should* come, that which is demanded, and insofar as it is demanded, it is realized only through human activity. In the tension of these two apparently contradictory factors lies the depth of the socialist principle. From this tension the theoretically most difficult and practically most important consequences follow. This tension corresponds precisely to the prophetic character of socialism, since the prophet is simultaneously one who demands and one who promises. What is proclaimed is the demanding will of God—not in the sense of a universal, timeless morality, but in the context of concrete, contemporary events. The prophet, from first to last, is linked with a unique situation, a situation that never recurs in precisely the same manner. The demands of the situation, therefore cannot be repeated either. It presses for a fulfillment that is unique. The prophetic demand concerns that toward which reality itself faces, that toward which a particular event is leading, that which is indicated by a certain constellation of factors, that which can be achieved—but also can fail of achievement. *This interpenetration of demand and promise characterizes all prophetic expectation. It is normative also for socialist expectation and identifies it unequivocally as prophetic.*[4] This is especially true of the Marxist interpretation of socialism (see below).

The fact that expectation is expectation of something that is demanded prevents it from being a passive waiting [*warten*], which really is not an *a*waiting [*erwarten*]. Even linguistically, *a*waiting is more than waiting in the manner of a passive spectator. Expectation includes action. Only an expectation that evokes action is genuine. If it had no effect on human activity, expectation would be an irrelevant theory.

Even the mythical consciousness of origin involves demand and action. But here the demand has a different character than it does in the prophetic and socialist context. In the context of the myth of origin, all demands aim at preserving the origin. All action seeks to realize what can be realized in the circular movement from the origin back to the origin. This demand does not reach out to the new, to that which transcends the origin. It confirms the origin, but does not go beyond it. It confirms the powers of origin, the feudal and priestly authorities.

The prophetic and socialist demand, by contrast, places every power, "high and low," under its scrutiny. Since it goes beyond that which pertains to the origin, it is independent of every pregiven power of being. This is the deeper meaning of egalitarianism, of *the demand for equality*, in prophetism and socialism. The inescapability of the demand, a demand that is addressed to everyone, makes all persons equal. That which one has, the fullness of one's being, with its luminous power, becomes insignificant in the presence of the unconditionality of the demand. Thereby the extraordinary possibility arises that human being may be fulfilled through the severest diminution of being. Hence the value that the prophetic and Christian viewpoint places on lowliness. In the same way, however, the demand arises that each person shall be treated in accordance with his or her destiny, that each person shall be allowed to enjoy the fullness of being without which, normally, one's humanity is destroyed. The ideal of maximal fulfillment of each person's being and the extreme case of a radical diminution of being are thus inclusive, and not exclusive, of each other.

For this reason the prophets fought against the repression of the poor by the powerful, and threatened the whole people with destruction on account of such injustice. *For this reason Marx fought against objectification and for a genuine humanism.* For this reason socialism views the proletarian situation as the crisis in bourgeois society and as the refutation of political romanticism. This struggle against oppression and exploitation by no means excludes the possibility that in a particular case the sacrifice even of one's very existence might be required. It does rule out, however, the right to defend an unjust form of domination by means of ideologies that glorify the situation of the poor and of the proletariat.[5]

4. Expectation and Origin

The concept of expectation unites origin and goal in a twofold way: the goal is the fulfillment of what is intended by the origin, while the origin engenders the power by which the goal is realized. These two aspects are of equal significance for the socialist movement. From the former, the content of socialist expectation is derived, from the latter, the way to its fulfillment.

Such a connection between origin and expectation is common to all types of expectation: the mythical, the prophetic, and the rationalistic. It is so deeply grounded in the concept itself that it prevails even where attempts are made to destroy it. A demand that has nothing to do with the being to which it is addressed has no rightful basis; it does not truly engage the one who is supposed to heed it. Likewise a promise that offers no fulfillment for the particular being to which it is given can neither be understood nor affirmed by this being. It does not concern him. Only that can be demanded and promised which brings fulfillment to the one to whom the demand or promise is addressed. Both therefore presuppose nonfulfillment. In mythical thought, this lack of fulfillment is viewed as the loss of an original perfection that must be recovered. For conceptual thought, the unfulfilled is the accidental, the unessential, which the essential will gradually overcome. The underlying motif is the same, as we see from the fact that reason itself has recourse to mythology. Rousseau and Marx, for example, speak of a "primitive communism," thus transposing the content of their expectation into the historical past, just as mythology does in envisioning a prehistorical, primal age.

From this correspondence between "primal time" and "end time" it follows that what is expected must have the features of the origin, even if these are altered by the movement of history that intervenes. The origin cannot be effaced in the fulfillment. This is true also for socialism and its expectation. The latter is not directed toward a form of being separated from the origin, as is the bourgeois principle. It is not directed toward a state of affairs in which being is abrogated, and then reconstituted by consciousness. It is directed, rather, toward the fulfillment of being. It strives toward being in its true power, with all its particularities, its tensions, and its forces of *eros*—not, however, as it is found prior to any question or demand; not as it rules unbrokenly, enslaving human consciousness and human society. Being comes to fulfillment only by transcending its immediate power. That is the heart of the prophetic and the socialist demand. That is the challenge they constantly direct against the powers of the unfulfilled origin. In the fulfillment, the origin returns, but it returns as something new; it is changed by the demand under which it stands. In this way the bourgeois principle is transcended in the socialist principle. The rights and the limits of the powers of origin are indicated. It thus becomes possible to resolve the inner conflict of socialism.

Origin and fulfillment are linked, secondly, in that the power of fulfillment stems from the origin. A mere demand that is addressed to being from somewhere beyond being has no intrinsic power. *The demand cannot move life if life itself is not moving in the direction of that which is demanded. A socialism of mere moralistic demand creates utopias, and is impotent against the actual forces of society.* Only when being moves itself toward its fulfillment can one speak of promise, and thus of expectation. On this point, too, mythology and conceptual thought are agreed. Myth speaks of events as directed by the powers of origin. In Jewish and Christian thinking, the symbol of providence is used in this connection, thereby expressing the unity of the "is" and the "ought." The notion of providence expresses the confidence that what is is not utterly removed from what should be; that in spite of the present lack of fulfillment, being is moving in the direction of fulfillment. One must keep the notion of providence apart from the childlike myths and childish distortions with which it has frequently been connected. Then what it says is that the Whence and Whither of existence are not split asunder; that the origin that bears us guarantees the realization of that which transcends it and yet in which it reaches its fulfillment.

Hegel's philosophy of history expresses the same notion. It is a faith in providence expressed in rational form. Hegel vehemently opposed a demand that is alien to being, a morality that violates life, a desire for world improvement that does not understand the depths of what is actually happening. Hegel spoiled his own concept by identifying a particular form of being as the tangible fulfillment of being. Thereby—in contradiction to the basic impulse of his thought—a particular spiritual and social configuration of history was equated with the goal of expectation. This form, i.e., the Prussian state after the Napoleonic wars, together with its religious, legal, and philosophical ramifications, no longer is subject to the demand. In it, the "is" and the "ought" become one. But the nerve of the religious concept of providence as well as of the Hegelian dialectic is thereby cut. The "ought" is swallowed up by the "is"; the powers of origin have escaped from the demand; the conservative form of political romanticism has triumphed.

Marx experienced and proclaimed the unfulfilled character of being—the same being that Hegel saw as fulfilled. The proletarian situation revealed to him what Hegel had not recognized—the internal split within the feudal-bourgeois system whose philosopher Hegel had been. Marx rejected Hegel's system and subjected it to the demand of justice. He gave expectation once again the role that it had in the prophetic tradition, in the belief in providence, and in the basic impulse of the Hegelian dialectic itself. Marx did not simply bypass Hegel and return to the Enlightenment, to moralism and utopianism. He rejected utopianism and "world improvement" as vigorously as did Hegel. For Marx, too, being must move in the direction of that which is demanded, so that the demand does not remain abstract and impotent. In his analysis of capitalist society these basic presuppositions receive concrete application and are elaborated by means of scientific methods. The structure of capitalism itself drives towards its transmutation into socialism, towards the classless society. *The socialist demand is confirmed by being itself.* The forces in the proletarian struggle, the revolt of primal humanity in the proletarian against the class situation, drive toward a socialist society. The promise of socialism grows out of the analysis of being itself. Marx set forth these ideas in terms of a purely economic analysis. In his later period, he no longer referred to the human factor, without which economics becomes a pure abstraction. Nonetheless the human dimension remained a tacit presupposition. The expectation of a "real humanism," as he had earlier called it, i.e., of a state of human fulfillment, is the driving power of all his scholarly investigations and political pronouncements.

The further questions that arise from Marx's integration of the "is" and the "ought" are dealt with below. What is decisive for the socialist principle is this integration as such, for it constitutes the second, and most important, bond between origin and goal. This above all makes socialist expectation an authentic expectation.

5. *The Prophetic and Rational Character of Expectation*

Socialism is a prophetic movement on the soil of autonomy and rationality. The prophetic substance is expressed in rational terms, both in knowledge and in action. This combination is essential for socialism. This is its uniqueness, its profundity and its peril. The way in which it constitutes a peril has already been indicated in our presentation of the inner conflict of socialism. This also, however, constitutes the profundity of socialism, the expression of its contemporaneity and authenticity, in contrast to the frivolous self-abnegation of autonomy and rationality in political romanticism.[6]

This combination of prophetic substance and rational form in socialism raises two sorts of questions. The one concerns socialism's goal, the other its means for reaching the goal. Insofar as expectation has a prophetic character, it transcends the known, the calculable, the manipulable aspects of being. It points to a new creation, something "wholly other." Insofar as expectation has a rational character, it remains within the dimension of the knowable. Here, too, it looks for something "other," but not "wholly other," since that which is coming stands in direct continuity with what is present now. *Prophetic expectation is transcendent; rational expectation is immanent.*

A similar contrast is found with respect to means. Insofar as expectation is prophetic, it reckons with the incalculable, which cannot be learned from the context of being. Insofar as expectation is rational, it seeks to eliminate the incalculable, and to unveil the powers of destiny as demonstrable and controllable causal sequences. *Prophetic expectation acknowledges factors in human life that are in principle incomprehensible; rational expectation, only factors that have not as yet been comprehended.*

The tension between these elements is indisputable and has had definite historical consequences. But the tension is not an opposition. Socialist thought and action is the reality of this tension, a tension that only becomes an opposition when living movement ceases. The socialist principle is too elastic to be destroyed by the tension between prophetic and rational expectation. Authentic human being transcends this opposition. *Human expectation is always transcendent and immanent at the same time. More precisely, this opposition does not exist for expectation.* Any study of prophetic eschatological expectation shows this clearly. The coming order of things is seen in historical continuity with the present; it is immanent. And yet, the concepts used to describe the coming order presuppose a total transformation of the present, a suspension of the laws of nature. The immanent is in fact transcendent. Or, the coming order is sundered from the present by an intervening world catastrophe; it is transcendent.

But the pictures by which all this is described are derived from the materials of everyday experience. The transcendent is in fact immanent. The same fluctuation can be found in the content of socialist expectation. It appears to be totally immanent: equality, freedom, the satisfying of human needs, etc. But when one examines the content of socialism's final expectation more closely, one finds that it presupposes a radical transformation of human nature, and in the last instance—since human nature constantly grows out of nature as such—a transformation of nature and its laws.

It is the same with the contrast between the incalculable and that which has yet to be calculated. The prophetic tradition, which clearly relies on the miraculous, nevertheless points to all the historical, political, and social factors that of necessity must lead to an event. Similarly paradoxical is the way in which an unwavering commitment to the socialist expectation can be combined with an awareness of the constantly changing character of all calculable factors—factors which are now propitious, now unpropitious for socialism. The reality of living expectation always and everywhere precedes an abstract analysis of its components. This is true both for prophetism and for socialism. Thus, "classless society" constitutes for socialism's basic approach to life just as much a transcendent symbol as an immanent object. Better still, one should say that it is neither the one nor the other, but rather that it shows the continual movement back and forth, the fluctuation and oscillation of real life. *Both prophetic and socialist expectation are a witness of life to its fundamental openness. They are a protest of life against false concepts of transcendence that inevitably call forth, in opposition, false concepts of immanence.*[7]

This is also true for socialism's perspective on the course of historical events and the factors that determine it. The " historical dialectic" is just as clearly a symbol as it is a rational concept. In it two notions vibrate—in the background a sense of transcendent destiny, and in the foreground historicoanalytical research and history-shaping policy. Neither inhibits the other. Even the most rigorously rational analysis contains within itself (not outside itself) an element that is inaccessible to it, not because it is too complex but because it cannot become the object of analysis. And even the strongest prophetic belief in providence never refrained from analyzing the real historical situation in detail and exhibiting its various factors. Any living historical consciousness, such as one finds in socialism, displays this kind of unity. The person oriented toward action assumes it at every moment. Only a type of thinking restricted to narrower categories would separate these elements. The tension between the prophetic and the rational elements in socialism is not a contradiction, but rather a genuine expression of a living expectation; it is that which constitutes its essence.

The socialist principle, the presentation of which is now completed, is a conceptual expression of the inner power of the socialist movement. It is the *dynamis* of socialism, captured in concepts and comprehended in a symbol. For this reason, and only for this reason, it is able to resolve socialism's conflict. However, before its power is tested by reference to the particular antinomies, we must discuss the relation between our understanding of the socialist principle and the basic self-understanding of the socialist movement, i.e., Marxism.

CHAPTER 6

The Socialist Principle and Problems of Marxism

1. The Problem of Historical Materialism

Marxism was the way in which the proletariat came to understand itself as a proletariat, and thereby to constitute itself as such. In Marxism the proletarian movement acquired its socialist self-consciousness. It is therefore no accident that political romanticism today wages its struggle against the proletarian movement as a struggle against Marxism. It is aided in this by the fact that Marxism itself has undergone basic changes that not only distort its image in the mind of the general public, but which also plunge it into the inner conflict of socialism. Any effort to comprehend the socialist principle in its essence and in its consequences must therefore be made in close relationship to this first and basic attempt at a conceptual exposition of socialism. Implicitly this has already been done in the preceding sections. Let us try once again, and this time explicitly. We shall approach the discussion in terms of two problems that can be called the central problems of Marxism—historical materialism and the historical dialectic.

Since the rise of metaphysical materialism near the end of the nineteenth century, the word *materialism* has acquired a sense that corresponds to Marxism as little as the accusation of materialistic thinking applies to the proletarian movement.[8] Neither the metaphysical nor the moral use of the word deals with the issue Marx was concerned with. The materialist interpretation of history is a concept that can only be understood when one establishes first of all its negative, and only then its positive significance. We have here a polemical concept [*Kampfbegriff*]. It developed in opposition to the idealist interpretation of history; its task was that of exposing historical idealism. While the idealist interpretation of history finds in history a directing logic, historical materialism abandons such a notion and seeks to find the real causes for the historical process. It identifies as the ultimate cause human nature, as determined by certain drives. But it sees human nature, in contrast to Feuerbach's notion of a universal, suprahistorical essence, as a historical reality that is indissolubly bound to a given social and economic context. *The "matter" of history, according to the materialistic interpretation, is consequently a humanity that seeks to satisfy its needs through a common productive enterprise.* With respect to the character of these needs and, consequently, the direction of the common productive enterprise, general statements can be made only insofar as a particular concept of human nature is assumed. For a theory will shape its assertions concerning the tendency and nature of the productive enterprise according to the image of human nature which that theory involves, whether consciously or unconsciously. At the same time, every doctrine of human nature must recognize that the immediate vital needs on which one's very existence depends are usually the most pressing. Were it otherwise, the survival of the human race down to the present would be inexplicable. If one chooses to call the acknowledgement of the urgency of these basic needs materialistic, then every interpretation of human nature and of history that deals with reality would have to be called materialistic. However, a doctrine that denies that in many specific instances the urgency of immediate vital needs is transcended is indeed materialistic, in the sense of a false, dogmatic conception. Such a conception does not acknowledge that even the most pressing needs are colored by their relationship to other needs, and by the specific historical situation in which this constellation of factors has come to be. Thus it is wrong to assert that human beings, at their lowest level, are animals, and that everything else is built upon this basis. Human life is not so mechanistic and lacking in structure. *Human beings are always human, even in the way in which their most vital needs are expressed,* whatever particular direction these may take or however they are related to the whole of human being. The "matter" of history is humanity, socially productive humanity. But this means real humanity, not an artificial construct, not a combination of animality and spirituality which does not show human traits in either dimension. Historical materialism thus has nothing to do with a materialistic doctrine of human nature. It only claims that the matter of history is socially productive humanity, not an overarching "reason."

But the notion of a materialist interpretation of history goes still further. It affirms the primacy of economics over other human functions. It makes the economic process the fundamental factor in historical development. The well-known doctrine of the substructure-superstructure relation between economics and the life of the spirit confirms this interpretation and gives it the power of a vivid image. The materialist interpretation of history, so understood, is an economic interpretation. *Materialism is economism.*

Marxism has hardly been attacked so vigorously for any other notion as for this one. It appeared to be a rejection of all so-called higher values, a rejection of the autonomy of love and truth, of justice and dedication. The system of bourgeois culture and religion—indeed, of all culture and religion—appeared to be threatened by this concept.

Here, too, a distinction must be made between the original, predominantly negative sense of the concept and its positive expression in terms of bourgeois thought. The distortion that the concept has suffered because of the inappropriate manner in which it was expressed is, to be sure, also attributable to Marx himself, and especially to Engels. However, as the picture of the young Marx now is becoming clearer, the meaning and purpose of his teaching is also becoming clearer. It is totally misleading to interpret the image of substructure-superstructure to mean that a discrete factor called "spirit" [*Geist*] is causally dependent on another discrete factor, "economics." Quite apart from the fact that the cause-effect relation is inappropriate to the image as well as to the matter itself, the very positing of two discrete factors, "economics" and "spirit," must be dismissed as nonsense. Economics is not a thing. It cannot even be conceived apart from the direction and quality of needs, the techniques of production and the social relationships involved, as well as the direction and scale of the productive enterprise. Economics is an infinitely complex, many-faceted reality. *All aspects of human being must be considered when economics is considered.* The latter cannot be isolated and made the cause of that which in fact is intrinsic to it, and without which it cannot be conceived.

It is just as impossible to posit spirit as a discrete factor and then to make it an effect of economics. This also is inherently inconceivable. *Spirit is never something in itself; it is always the spirit of something, the spirit of a being that, through spirit, achieves self-understanding.* Marx saw this connection between being and consciousness very clearly and laid strong emphasis upon it. Precisely this unity is lost, however, when being is conceived as the cause from which spirit follows as an effect. There is no such being and no such spirit.

The notion of reflection as in a mirror thus is also inadequate to explain the relation between being and consciousness, or between economics and the spirit. Using that image involves the assumption that there is an entity that is what it is, quite apart from its reflection. A person, to be sure, is independent of the physical mirror in which he sees his image. But human being is not independent of human consciousness. Human being is always twofold being, a unity of being and consciousness. *Social being apart from social consciousness is a meaningless concept*, for the being of society is inseparably bound to consciousness.

Socialism faces a challenge at the level of fundamental theory —the challenge of freeing the question of the relation of being to consciousness, of economics to the world of spiritual forms, from primitive distortions that turn them into nonsense, and of taking a fresh approach to the problem, following Marx's lead. In this connection it is most important to clarify the polemical significance that the *concept of ideology* had for Marx, a matter that must not be forgotten when one employs this concept to probe the relationship of being and consciousness. The fact that consciousness is always bound to being does not mean that a specific false consciousness cannot arise in particular social situations, i.e., a discrepancy between inherited concepts and symbols and a new historical reality.[9] But since historical reality means the reality of the whole person, including the realm of thought, a false consciousness can only appear in a society if a true consciousness is also present, namely a consciousness that is united with the new being, which alone makes this consciousness possible. *A false consciousness is nothing other than the willful self-affirmation of old social structures that are being threatened and destroyed by new ones.* True and false in this context, therefore, means agreeing or not agreeing with the underlying structures of a social order. Marxism has expressed the extent to which the bourgeoisie has concealed from itself its own actual structure. The hostility of bourgeois society against the exposure of capitalism is therefore necessary and natural, even if unjustified.

Yet there must be some restraint on the unbridled appetite for such exposure which has frequently characterized Marxism. A symbolic world is "ideological" in the sense of false consciousness only when there are no real structures corresponding to it. Now our analysis of bourgeois society has shown that the bourgeoisie is in fact supported by prebourgeois* forces, that the bourgeois principle serves as a corrective and a disturbance to prebourgeois society, rather than simply its replacement. *There is no warrant, therefore, for denouncing all prebourgeois elements in bourgeois society as expressions of a false consciousness.* Neither can the concepts and symbols of revolutionary political romanticism be dealt with in this way. To dismiss them, as is commonly done, as the ideology and false consciousness of certain middle-class groups cannot account for their success. The genuine meaning and the ideological misuse of a concept can interpenetrate each other in a most complex way. Powers related to the myth of origin can be made to serve bourgeois society; concepts and

* Correction; the text reads "bourgeois."—TRANS.

symbols derived from the myth of origin can be used in a way that completely contradicts their inherent meaning. Thus they are not ideological in themselves, but their employment in the service of bourgeois society gives them an ideological function.

The charge that the bourgeois belief in harmony was ideological insofar as it served to obscure the actual situation of the proletariat, on the other hand, was fully vindicated. The demonstration of the disharmony in bourgeois society, i.e., *the exposure of the class situation, was the most significant and most effective accomplishment of the Marxist theory of ideology.* It was in this way that the socialist principle was first understood, that the proletariat reached self-awareness, and that the proletarian struggle attained world historical significance. The materialistic interpretation of history, therefore, remains an essential and inseparable part of socialism as long as the latter is involved in the struggle with bourgeois society. But its validity extends even further. *Socialism has permanent cause to suspect itself of being an ideology.* Wherever socialism, in contradiction to its own nature, has adopted the bourgeois belief in harmony, where it dwells in illusions and seeks to conceal its own inner tensions, it stands in need of a theory of ideology directed against itself.[10]

The socialist principle, in having the power to resolve the conflict of socialism, also has the power to deal with the problems of historical materialism and to provide a new basis for the concept of ideology. The way in which this must occur depends above all on socialism's new understanding of human nature.

2. The Problem of the Historical Dialectic

The second problem that Marxism poses is the historical dialectic. This is determinative particularly for the relationship between Marxism and the proletarian movement, since the historical dialectic furnishes the theory of this movement. In our exposition of the socialist principle, the unity of the "is" and the "ought," of the movement of history and the demand for action, has already been discussed. It also has been shown how living expectation contains both elements, and how expectation transcends the contradiction that results from the use of inappropriate categories. But the problem this tension poses is not thereby resolved. The theory of the historical dialectic is an attempt at a solution; and since it has had such an incalculable practical effect on the socialist movement, we are compelled to state our position on this issue.

There are two questions that must be considered. First, there is the question concerning the character of that movement of being with which the demand must remain in accord. Secondly, there is the question of the relation of human action to this movement of being. One can describe the problem in brief as the question of the relation between necessity and freedom in the achievement of socialism. One must, however, be careful about importing into the discussion a particular concept of necessity or freedom, thus obstructing from the start one's understanding of historical dialectic.

In the prophetic tradition, as in Hegel and Marx, one finds the peculiar notion that history moves forward toward its goal, as it were, *behind the backs of the bearers of historical action.* Movements among the Gentiles whose participants do not know Yahweh nonetheless are subject to his control and derive their meaning from what they signify for Israel. Even the destruction of Israel's political existence by the world powers is the work of Yahweh, carried out for the sake of the demand and promise given to his people. The Gentiles must fulfill the will of Yahweh apart from or even contrary to their knowledge and their will. Finally, they thereby serve themselves as well—against their will —since through Israel the unity of the human race will be effected, the end toward which all history moves.

Hegel taught that the meaning of history is fulfilled through the passions, especially of great historical personalities, without their knowledge or will. The "cunning of reason" consists in its using the passions in order to achieve its own purposes. Passions may appear to drive the individual or the nations arbitrarily; actually, they serve the logic of history.

According to Marx, the development of a capitalist economy, quite contrary to the knowledge and intention of its bearers, leads to its transmutation into a classless society. To be sure, each particular act of capitalistic economic aspiration, each technical improvement, each concentration of finance and industry directly serves the capitalistic competitive system. But each also leads indirectly to the abrogation of capitalism. According to Marx too, therefore, moral reason is realized through a process which contradicts the intentions of its bearers.

In all three cases, what is moves toward what ought to be without the demand being championed by conscious human action, indeed often in opposition to all human knowing and willing.

What sort of necessity is this that asserts itself behind the back of human arbitrariness? In an objectified world, necessity can signify only *subjection to the law of cause and effect* and *calculability*. If Marx and the historical dialectic are interpreted on this basis, there arises the kind of Marxism which was active at the end of the nineteenth century and later, and which, more than anything else, shattered the power of socialist action. In the face of calculable necessity, one can only act in a calculating manner—making predictions, gathering corroborating evidence, closely observing the gauge of progress, and making entries about the stage of development that has been reached—activities to which especially Marxist intellectuals love to devote themselves. What was demonstrated thereby was that the predictions concerning the technical organization of capitalism, concerning business cycles and crises, were accurate to a high degree; but what for socialism is the decisive factor, the human response to these developments, was judged wholly incorrectly. The proletariat, the bourgeoisie, and political romanticism behaved differently than should have been the case according to the primitive understanding of human nature held by these theoreticians. This came as a shock to the representatives of socialist theory. Marx's incidental observation that barbarism as well as socialism could arise at the end of capitalist development was raised to a dogmatic utterance of the first rank.

The necessity and calculability of history and of the development of capitalism were placed in question. Human action was made the decisive factor. Freedom took the place of necessity.

The motif of "ethical socialism," which had been displaying ever greater strength within Western socialism, covered over the Marxist foundation. The spirit of youth rebelled against the spectator attitude. Political passion freed itself from the fetters of mere theoretical contemplation. One dared again to confront reality with demands for which one could find no basis in reality itself. The utopian form of socialism began to gain power—and with it, the arbitrariness and fortuitousness of the demand, the tendency toward romanticism, the overestimate of the thinking and willing of individuals, and alienation from the movement of the masses.[11]

The dialectical method was just as grievously misunderstood in this way as it had been earlier in terms of the doctrine of necessity. The theory fluctuated between opposites, both of which were equally far removed from reality. The theory of necessity viewed humanity and history in terms of the model of a thing possessing attributes, and thus landed in insoluble contradictions. Where reality is viewed as a thing, freedom is excluded, for a thing is totally conditioned. Freedom, however, contains within itself an element of unconditionality. On the other hand, freedom had to be affirmed for the sake of the demand, which in the situation of political struggle one did not dare abandon even for an instant. This contradiction can only be resolved and *the dialectic can only be understood when the model of a thing is abandoned.* Human being and human history must be understood as they really present themselves. They must not be misrepresented as abstract things; even though this may be necessary for special purposes, it never captures the whole reality. The picture of humanity and of history that emerges, unfalsified by the use of a pregiven category, is different. History cannot be calculated, for it contains within itself the possibility of the new. But neither is it dependent on the whim of free human action. History has within itself a directionality, an impetus. *Always and everywhere, it travels the road from the bond of origin to the final fulfillment.* But it moves on this way through human *action.* If it were to bypass human action, there could be no fulfillment, for apart from human action, being is neither fulfilled nor unfulfilled; it lies beneath that contrast. The fulfillment of being is fulfilled human action that corresponds to the demand. No miracle nor any natural process can produce the fulfillment of being if human action is bypassed.

But the opposite is also true: the fulfillment of being is not dependent on human arbitrariness. It is the inner meaning and the aim of every particular historical process. It is the impulse of history in each of its moments. Again, this does not mean, however, that history can be viewed as an objective process that will inevitably reach its goal, a goal which thus would be locatable in time and space. That is utopianism, and such an interpretation of history is utopian in all its parts. The impulse of history cannot be converted into a succession of external events. What actually takes place contradicts the impulse of history just as much as it corresponds to it. *There is no universal history as a theodicy, demonstrating the successful transmutation of the "ought" into the "is."*

The historical dialectic—the unity of the movement of being and the demand—therefore cannot imply making human action, including the struggle for socialism, dependent on particular findings concerning the present social situation, the prevailing balance of power, economic trends, or the probability of victory for this or that group. Socialist action proceeds from the inner conviction that it corresponds to the meaning and impulse of history. For it is concerned with the fulfillment of the origin in the goal, understood in terms of the contemporary situation. It is the prophetic movement of our time; it is the movement that places itself under the demand of justice. It can only be the task of theory to develop this thought, both in principle, as has been done here, and in terms of factual particulars, as Marx attempted to do. It is important to realize that human being itself requires that the origin be made subordinate to the demand. It is important also, if barbarism is to be avoided, to recognize the forces in contemporary capitalist society that drive towards socialism. This is not just tactically important, in order to make it possible to initiate action on the basis of a correct estimate of the human and historical factors involved (this would still be an undialectical way of thinking). It is also necessary because an action can meet with success only if it corresponds with being, and because only that demand can evoke and sustain victorious passion which is certain that reality itself is on its side. The enormous significance of Marxism for the proletarian struggle was that it offered such assurance. And this assurance is in no way weakened by the coexisting threat of another outcome, namely, chaos and barbarism. Popular Marxism wasted this power by turning the dialectic into a method of calculation, a calculation that is forever changing and is constantly a source of disappointment. "Ethical socialism" can never evoke this power, because it presents a demand that is unrelated to being and is not one with the impulse of history.

We must press our argument to an even deeper level, one that was already prefigured by Marx. It might seem that knowledge of human being, of history, and of the dynamics of the present could be won by pure contemplation, detached from action. But this is not the case. The relation does not proceed in a one-sided manner from knowledge to action, but also from action to knowledge. *It is not from just any locus in history that one can learn the interrelation between human being, historical reality, and the socialist demand.* There is at present one favored place for this: the proletarian situation. Here the ideologies with which the bourgeoisie and political romanticism disguise the class situation are exposed, forcefully exposed. The proletariat can camouflage nothing, for it stands on the negative side of the social ledger. It experiences directly, in its own existence, the injustice of the social structure. It reacts directly against this injustice, and lives directly in the expectation of, and experiences the tension towards a new order of things, towards justice. What in any other place happens only through reflection, and therefore by chance, happens here of necessity and without rational argumentation. What in any other place is possible only for individuals—to see through the social ideologies—happens here among the masses without any effort, through their sheer existence. The natural, instinctive reactions themselves drive towards justice. Therefore, the decision for socialism occurs less by chance among the proletariat than at any other place. It develops directly out of the concrete historical situation. It is demanded, as it were, by the situation itself. Marx thus correctly brought socialist knowledge and action into primal connection with the proletariat. The fact that we find here a place where socialism, with dialectical necessity, grows out of being itself, constitutes the starting point for socialism's proof of the historical dialectic as a whole. The "is" and the "ought" are thus linked together once again in a concrete human situation. The socialist demand and historical reality are as one in the knowledge and action of the proletariat. At the same time, a structure of human being as such is disclosed in such thought and action, thus demonstrating that socialism is the decisive concern of Western humanity as a whole.

3. Critique of Dogmatic Marxism

The foregoing interpretation and development of the problems of Marxism as well as the overall assessment of socialism presented here must be defended against a kind of dogmatic Marxism that rejects out of hand the questions and concepts that have figured in our analysis. This kind of Marxism regards any discussion of the problems of human nature and society, of culture and education, of expectation and demand, as so much superfluous or harmful ideology. In the prerevolutionary period, the theoretician is required to give an analysis of the then current social situation while the practical leaders (among whom the theoreticians must also be counted) must pursue revolutionary action. Other questions will presumably disappear after the victorious revolution, or else will answer themselves. This perspective has a power that can be very stimulating, especially when combined with a resolute and dedicated revolutionary praxis. It is especially persuasive when, rejecting the inconclusiveness of endless theoretical discussions, it calls for the acceptance of a few basic dogmas, and for the rest, praxis. The impact of Communism especially on the younger intellectuals is attributable to this decisive and basically nontheoretical attitude.

But the history of the German Communist party shows that, at

least in Germany, things do not work out this way. The doctrinal
basis is too weak to support a successful praxis. It has proved to
be neither theoretically penetrating nor practically illuminating.
The suppression of urgent theoretical questions, combined with a
dogmatic narrowness and hardness, can indeed strengthen the
cohesiveness of a group externally, but it will weaken and falsify
its inner life.

Therefore the present study concerns itself with questions such
as these: What practical significance can analyses of contemporary society have? To what extent is the historical process calculable? What would a socialist praxis look like? What is the
nature of the human being with whom the revolution has to
deal—proletarian, bourgeois, and prebourgeois? What are the
real motivating forces of the socialist movement and its countermovements? What accounts for their strengths and weaknesses?
We must discuss the role that expectation plays in the proletarian
struggle, both positively through the psychological powers that it
awakens, and negatively through the psychological letdown that
every disappointed expectation brings in its train. *All this is intended to extricate Marxism from the dogmatic narrowness into
which it has fallen among the epigoni, and to restore it to the
breadth it had in the young Marx*, and which "the Marx of *Das
Kapital*" had not abandoned in principle, but only in order to
narrow the scope of his own work.[12] This certainly gave his
dogmatically inclined followers a convenient pretext for ignoring
the broader problems he had treated earlier. It is in the realm of
these problems, however, that the presuppositions for any assertion of an economic Marxism have their locus. The fact that these
presuppositions were accepted uncritically or were spoiled by
primitivization has to a considerable extent determined the fate
of German socialism. It is possible to demonstrate down to the
smallest detail the inner connection between socialist action in
Germany and the uncritical adoption of what were for Marx
himself the unexpressed presuppositions of his economic analysis.
This is true in fact, and it is true also for the caricature that
political romanticism has made of Marxism, a caricature that it
could use to extraordinary effect, with politically disastrous re-

sults. It is dogmatic Marxism that is primarily responsible for this caricature, not Marx himself, except perhaps to a limited extent.

It is common knowledge that a dogmatician dreads nothing more than a discussion of his own unstated presuppositions. He seeks to avoid this by disputing his opponent's right even to enter into the discussion, or by regarding any such discussion as already prejudiced against him. Thus the orthodox believer refuses to discuss the presuppositions of his faith, while the occultist likewise refuses to discuss the presuppositions of his visions. For no discussion that is not based upon such faith or visions would, it is claimed, be able to deal at all with the subject matter that is supposed to be discussed. In the same way, the dogmatic Marxist refuses to discuss the presuppositions of his dogmas. He castigates counterarguments as bourgeois ideology, without the least suspicion that he himself could be captive to an ideology. He postpones any decision on this matter until the day when the victorious revolution will have proven him correct. The discussion is ended with a demand that one put oneself at the disposal of the revolution, and that means in practice, at the disposal of dogmatic Marxism. Thus dogmatic Marxism, like every dogmatically rigid system, demands a radical leap. One who has not made the leap is in no position to criticize the system, while one who has made it no longer engages in such criticism.

CHAPTER 7

The Resolution of Socialism's Inner Conflict through the Unfolding of the Socialist Principle

Introduction: The Proletariat and Revolutionary Romantic Groups

The socialist principle is able to resolve the inner conflict of socialism. But since the conflict of socialism is rooted in the conflict of the proletarian situation, such a solution must be based on an overcoming of the conflict in the proletarian situation. The socialist principle is able to resolve socialism's antinomies only when, and to the extent that, it serves as the expression of powers in the proletarian movement through which the proletariat's own antinomies are overcome.

The source of the inner conflict in the proletarian situation is the twofold relation of the proletariat to bourgeois society: the need simultaneously to fulfill and to oppose the bourgeois principle. Thus it proved impossible to win victory over the bourgeois principle by means of the bourgeois principle. Since every attack on the principle operated on the latter's own grounds and with its own weapons, each attack has actually served to strengthen what was attacked. The situation was made still worse by the fact that prebourgeois forces that could have been deployed in the struggle had long since been co-opted by the bourgeoisie, and therefore were not available to the proletariat as possible allies. And yet such an attack can be launched only with the participation of the powers of origin. *The power of origin in the proletariat that revolts, psychologically, against objectification through the bourgeois principle must at the same time find expression, sociologi-*

cally, in origin-related groups that fight against bourgeois domination. The psychological and sociological dimensions correspond, and only if the psychological dimension related to the origin among the proletariat is coordinated with the sociological dimension related to the origin in the nation as a whole, can socialism be realized at present. Such coordination was impossible as long as the origin-related prebourgeois groups were allied with the bourgeoisie for the preservation of class domination. This alliance compelled the proletariat on its part to radicalize the bourgeois principle.

As long as this situation lasted, socialism attempted in vain to establish an alliance with peasants, artisans, and public officials in opposition to capitalist domination. Because of its specifically proletarian connections, socialism has not grasped the significance of the bond of origin that does exist among those groups, however lax that bond might be. Consequently, socialist theory has involved a constant mixture of true and false elements. It has correctly seen that these groups can be integrated into the socialist struggle only if rationalism has freed them from the unbroken bond of origin. On the other hand, it has been mistaken in demanding that these groups must actually become proletarianized, in the sense of a total assimilation into the class situation of the proletariat. That certainly has not happened so far, and there is no assurance that it ever will. It *could* happen; there are important signs, such as the rationalization of agriculture, which indicate that it is happening. If this did occur, a unified proletarian attack on capitalism would be possible. The powers of origin resident in the proletariat would be immensely strengthened by these newly enlisted masses, which were until just recently at a prebourgeois level. But it may also turn out differently, and a great deal at the present time suggests just this. Indeed it is possible, and it is partly already the case, that the net income of these groups may fall below the level of the industrial proletariat. Social and psychological structures, however, are not unequivocally determined by levels of income.[13] The question of whether the victory of socialism will occur through a general proletarianization of all nonbourgeois groups within the nation must be left open. It cannot be decided at this time. *But it is certain that in the face of the present situation, we cannot afford to wait for the general proletarianization of society. We must strive instead for an alliance of the revolutionary proletariat with the revolutionary groups within political romanticism.*

The new and pivotal factor in the present situation is that the origin-related groups have assumed, to a large extent, a stance of opposition to bourgeois society. It is the function of National Socialism to have accomplished this revolution by means that corresponded to the origin-related character of these groups. Prerequisite to this success was, to be sure, the shattering of the mutually supportive relationship of the bourgeois and the pre-bourgeois forces through which they maintained the system of class dominion at the expense of the proletariat. The World War, the inflation, and the international economic crisis forced the bourgeoisie to impose the cost of dominion upon the middle classes, too. They were sucked into the crisis of capitalism, not only as individuals but also as groups. For a time, capitalism had held out advantages for them: the possibility of appointment and promotion as clerks and middle-level officials in the bureaucracy; strong safeguards against unemployment; the management of, and payment of interest on, savings; the heavy demand especially for products created by advanced agricultural methods. But all this perished in the war, the inflation, and the economic crisis. Thereby a new situation was created for socialism. It is not mere demagoguery for the revolutionary movement of the middle classes to call itself socialist. It has a real "expectation." The symbolic term *the Third Reich*, for example, refers not only to the concept of a third German empire; it also, by virtue of the magic number three, conjures up the ancient expectations of a third age. The content of this expectation is simply the unbroken origin, reflecting the inner contradiction of political romanticism in general. Thus the movement is in constant danger of being absorbed by the conservative form of political romanticism and of being led back into the service of class rule. This danger is all the greater since the movement's *Führer* appears to be working for this end. If this should happen, the realization of socialism in

Germany would be impossible, unless new movements should arise out of economic or political catastrophies. Since socialist expectation does not involve the making of predictions, it does not enable us to decide the issue one way or another. It is open to both possibilities. Socialist expectation does not require the proletarianization of the middle classes; it can enter into an alliance with them even if such a proletarianization does not take place. The socialist principle opens up the possibility of such an alliance. This call to make use of this possibility is part of the socialist decision that is demanded here and now.[14]

1. Origin and Goal in the Expectation of the Future

The internal conflict in socialist belief is resolved by the socialist principle. This conflict stems from the fact that socialism adopted and radicalized the bourgeois conception of the world while rejecting the underlying bourgeois belief in harmony. Socialism was thus forced to posit a future reality that could not be understood at all as an extrapolation from the present. It had to reckon with an absolute leap; but this came close to being a belief in miracles, which of course contradicted its own presuppositions.

Socialist expectation receives from the socialist principle a content that resolves its inner conflict. What is expected is not an absolute contradiction of present reality, but rather, it is the true meaning of the origin. What is demanded is not some abstract norm of justice unrelated to the origin, but rather the fulfillment of the origin itself.

The concept of a classless society, therefore, does not imply a society cut off from the power of origin. Also in the society which socialism wishes to create, the factors of soil, blood, and social group will be present. Also in this society, traditions and symbols understood by everyone will be found, as well as faith and devotion. It is these very forces, both in the proletariat and among the revolutionary origin-related groups, that are resisting class rule as we know it today. Through them alone can the classless society be realized. For only that which can sustain itself victoriously in the struggle for a classless society has constitutive significance for the classless society. The means and the end are not separable, as is supposed by utopians and those who believe in miracles.

Thus for example, socialism cannot win its social victory without the support of aggressive groups ready for ultimate sacrifice, or without the support of extraordinarily powerful individuals. The inner differentiations within the socialist movement, the formation of vanguards and leadership groups, therefore, are regrettable only from the standpoint of an abstract socialism that has fallen prey to the bourgeois principle.[15] For an authentic socialist movement, everything depends on whether and to what extent such differentiation occurs.

Similarly, the inner differentiations within the working class, the advanced character of particular trade unions, and the national and regional peculiarities of the proletariat are not necessarily a threat to the socialist movement. The underlying forces of the socialist movement, and hence of the future classless society as well, articulate themselves in these groups. *Thereby the structure of the classless society is being prepared.*

The place that the groups representing revolutionary political romanticism will occupy within this structure depends on whether they enter it as they are, without first having to go through a radical proletarianization. If they do enter as origin-related groups the tensions remaining between them and the proletariat can lead to fruitful political developments, as in Russia.

With this kind of self-understanding, socialist belief is freed from being caught in the antinomy between radical pessimism concerning the present and radical optimism concerning the future, or between a rational conception of the world and a highly irrational belief in miracles. A belief in harmony in the sense of the bourgeois principle, to be sure, is ruled out. Opposition among the powers of origin can never cease; and such opposition does involve the danger of violence and oppression. The factor of space and the coexistence it implies are not abolished and should not be. All the same, socialism can overcome and eliminate from a vast stretch of human history any blanket approval of the powers of origin simply as they are. Socialism can address the challenge of justice to that which is, to that which is powerful. Socialist belief is as far from the pessimism of a conservative Lutheranism that submits without protest to the existing demonic powers, as it is from the optimism of the bourgeois principle that believes in an automatic harmony.

This is why socialism, at least in principle, must look beyond itself and its own achievement of a new social order. Socialism is not the end of socialism's striving. To be sure, socialist belief is historically dependent on the prophetic expectation of a millennium, but it transcends the utopian form that this belief assumed under the domination of the bourgeois principle. It is precisely at this point that religious socialism has tried to penetrate and purify socialist belief. Through the concept of the *kairos,* it has attempted to clarify the limits as well as the validity and meaning of concrete expectation.[16] Expectation as such, expectation as a human attitude, comes into being in terms of a definite content of expectation pertinent to a particular time. *Expectation is always bound to the concrete, and at the same time transcends every instance of the concrete.* It possesses a content that is dependent on the spiritual or social group involved, yet it transcends this content. The vitality and depth of socialist faith lies in the fact that it so distinctly—and so dangerously—embodies this tension. For the most perilous posture one can assume is that of expectation.

2. *Being and Consciousness in the Picture of Human Nature*

The antinomy of the socialist view of human nature was rooted in the fact that socialism conceived of human nature from the standpoint of reason. Socialism expected that reason would prove victorious, whether in a liberal or a democratic mode. But, at the same time, socialism abandoned the idea of harmony upon which this expectation was grounded. So it had to posit a leap from a present irrational situation to a future rational situation. This contradiction had fateful consequences for socialism's image of those who were to be its supporters, as well as of those who fought against it.

The socialist principle resolves this antinomy by pointing to the powers of origin in human life. The first step toward a new socialist understanding of human nature is the *repudiation of the primitive "drive psychology"* on which vulgar Marxism built its calculations of the future. The notion that human being could be conceived as a mechanism whose driving power is simply a primitive reaction to pleasure and pain resulted in a mechanistic conception according to which, as the suffering of the increasingly proletarianized masses became greater and greater, a pain-reaction would result that would touch off the revolution. Also completely primitive and removed from reality was the notion, derived from the liberal belief in harmony, that after the victory of the revolution, a universal and uniform satisfaction of human needs would prevail.

The human person is not a mechanism determined by simple pleasure and pain reactions. That notion is an extreme product of bourgeois objectification, both in concept and in actuality. A person constructed in this way would indeed be a thing, and not a person. He or she would really be nothing more than that which in the bourgeois system one is supposed to be: a commodity called "labor power," a cog in the machinery of production. If this image of humanity, particularly as applied to the proletariat, were correct, there could be no proletarian movement, nor any such thing as socialism. To the extent that this image is applicable —to the extent, that is, that class domination has in fact succeeded in turning persons into things—there are certainly calculable pain-reactions, reactions against momentarily excessive pressure; but there is no socialism, nor are there any forces to fight for it or to support it. For socialism is precisely the counter-movement against this process of dehumanization, against the tendency of capitalism to turn people into psychological mechanisms possessing calculable pleasure-pain reactions. The socialist concept of human nature has set forth at the level of theory an image of the human against the practical consequences of which the whole socialist movement is directed: the person who has become a thing.

Socialism must understand the human person in terms of his or her spiritual and vital center. This must be done, however, not in the fashion of a vitalistic philosophy that robs humanity of what is uniquely human, the "doubling" of being in consciousness, but rather in accordance with the socialist principle, i.e., the subordination of the origin to the demand. Even in human beings so understood there are mechanisms. It is as necessary for any psychology as for any political praxis to know and reckon with these mechanisms. But the fact that there are mechanisms at play in a living being does not make that being itself a mechanism. Here lies the basic error of the objectified interpretation of the world that even socialism has not avoided, in spite of its protest against it.

This insight into the inadequacies of the older socialist concept of human nature has led today in many places to an *alliance of Marxism and psychoanalysis*.[17] The attempt is being made to overcome the mistakes of the older interpretation of human nature by a profounder and more complex psychology. These efforts are important and welcome. Psychoanalysis, however has two aspects. On the one hand, it is oriented to the nineteenth century, and works with concepts and notions that correspond to the mechanical, objectified interpretation of the world expressed by the bourgeois principle. If this aspect of psychoanalytic research is made central, there is some improvement, to be sure, but no fundamental change in the vulgar Marxist view. *The psychology of drives is refined, but the basic understanding of human nature is not altered.* However, there is another side to psychoanalysis. It dethrones consciousness and shatters faith in its supremacy. It points to the forces of the psychic and vital center that determine consciousness, even when the latter believes itself to be self-sufficient and capable of making free decisions. Psychoanalysis opens up access to levels, the exposure of which profoundly threatens mechanistic psychology. Above all it points to connections between spiritual forms and the vitalities of life, a connection that corresponds to the authentic Marxist view of history, undistorted by bourgeois influence. These matters are unresolved at present. What is important is that with the introduction of psychoanalysis, the struggle for a new understanding of human nature is beginning, even in the radical Marxist camp.

When persons are understood in terms of their vital and psychic center, a series of important consequences result for appraising the proletarian movement and its countermovements. First of all, an anthropological basis is provided for the Marxist notion that the terminus of capitalism could be barbarism as well as socialism. Even if the economic mechanism performs as Marxist theory indicates (and since it has, by definition, a technical character, is in fact a mechanism, and hence to a considerable extent is calculable), nothing is determined thereby concerning human reactions, either those of the proletariat or those of other groups. Even a knowledge of all previous economic and psychological factors would not settle the matter. For it is the nature of the origin to posit something original, which in turn posits something original, and so on. Since all living beings, including human beings, are rooted in an origin, human life is not determined by a fixed number of impersonal factors whose present and future combinations could be calculated. To be sure, positivism is right in refusing to be dissuaded from the task of establishing causal relationships and predicting the future on the basis of them, by opponents who appeal to the limits of knowledge, to intuition and irrationality. *The methodological demand for rational analysis must remain unquestioned.* The required breaking of the myth of origin is largely dependent on this principle. But positivism is wrong when it makes an ontological thesis out of a methodological requirement, thus reducing being as such to a conglomeration of objective and calculable components. There is no justification for such an inference. It contradicts itself and it contradicts reality.[18]

Furthermore, the new understanding of human nature implies a new theory of needs. Since all types of human penetration into reality are grounded in the inner layer of human being that we have called the "center," and since all needs likewise have their roots here, it is not possible to isolate certain needs and derive the remaining ones from them. To be sure, we must acknowledge the priority of the instinct of self-preservation in most living beings; but this priority takes effect only in situations in which life itself is threatened. In most cases, the actual life-process knows nothing of such a priority. Life is made up of a complex of vital, erotic, aesthetic, and religious impulses that in many instances lead to an ascendancy of so-called "spiritual" impulses over the life-preserving tendencies. (Cf. the dedication even unto death of members of the fighting proletariat.) But even this formulation is questionable since in many cases the drive toward self-preservation is by no means concerned with "life at any price," but rather with a specific quality of life, e.g., life in freedom. Even such basic needs as hunger and thirst are inwardly complex. Apart from extreme cases of direst need which press one beyond the limits of human consciousness, the need for food and clothing and the like is also infinitely differentiated and determined by vital, aesthetic, and erotic elements, whose reciprocal effect causes radical changes even in the spheres of the most primitive need-satisfaction. A better *theory of needs* would help to explain both the changes and differentiations within the proletariat itself, and the fact that the middle classes reject proletarian forms of existence even when they are at a lower economic level than the proletariat. (The phrase "white-collar proletariat" is not just a caricature, it is also an expression of a real and justifiable tendency within human being.) Yet further consequences of the changed concept of human nature will be indicated as we deal with the remaining antinomies. They will demonstrate the fundamental significance that a new interpretation of human nature has for all aspects of socialist theory and praxis. It can truly be said that socialism's dependence on the bourgeois principle in its view of human nature has proved to be most disastrous for its own development. A decisive change in this respect is basic to the socialist decision that we now confront.

One point remains to be dealt with in this connection: the domination of the conscious mind, as this corresponds to the bourgeois principle. The work of enlightenment that socialism has performed among the proletariat (and which it has attempted in vain among the middle classes) has proved decisive for the self-understanding of the proletariat as a proletariat, for the spiritual superiority of even simple proletarians over most of their bourgeois and prebourgeois antagonists, and for the determined and disciplined manner in which proletarians have conducted the class struggle. But this enlightenment has also had other consequences that are negative in character. It failed to make clear *the difference between the matters themselves and their ideological misuse*. The powers and symbols of origin were attacked because of the misuse to which they were subjected in the interest of class domination. But socialists neglected to point out their original and authentic use, and their basic significance for human being and for the coming society. In this way the estrangement from the origin emerged that outwardly characterizes the proletariat, but which in fact contradicts its fight against objectification. For the proletarian movement draws its fighting power not from the enlightenment of individual proletarians, but from that in the origin which is back of the rational forms through which it expresses itself. It is not the most enlightened, the so-called "most progressive" consciousness that influences history. It is the consciousness whose energies flow from the fullness and depth of being, which it brings to light. Such energies are often lacking among socialist intellectuals. As a result, its very high degree of enlightenment and its amazingly progressive consciousness are neither symbolically powerful nor historically creative. The excessive influence of such elements in socialism must be counterbalanced by the release of the powers of origin within the proletariat, and by the assimilation of these same powers as they are found outside the proletariat. All this clearly presupposes a view of human nature quite different from that which socialism took from the bourgeois principle, in contradiction to its own principle.

3. *Power and Justice in the Structuring of Society*

The antinomy of most direct importance for politics, that found in the socialist concept of society, is expressed in the contradictory and inwardly uncertain attitude of socialism to power and to the state. On the one hand, it feels compelled to reject both power and the state in the name of a radically consistent rational principle; on the other hand, it is constrained to affirm them both in order to achieve the realization of socialism. It is just here that socialism must accomplish what is for it the most difficult, but politically the most important, transformation. It must break through to a positive understanding of power and from there to a new theory of the state.

A theory of power that corresponds to the socialist principle must be derived from the relationship of power to the origin and goal of human life.[19] Power is related to ability, capability. One who has power is able to prevail over those who are subject to this power. Power implies the relatively constant possibility of prevailing in this manner. The first question, then, is this: In what is such a capability, such a fixed possibility, grounded? What is the underlying basis for power?

The possibility of social power is based in the necessity of creating a unified social will. A unified will, however, comes to expression only through a leading group, or through individuals designated by the group, in whom this unity is represented and through whom it is expressed. *Thus power is the actualization of social unity.* Tendencies toward fragmentation are overcome by the entity possessing power, and opposing forces are brought into subjection. One will is created out of many.

This general presupposition for social power does not yet, however, suggest the reasons why a particular group can exercise power or supply the bearers of power. This can only be understood in terms of the social superiority of the group in question. Its superiority can be expressed in various ways: magical, military, economic, cultural, etc. The group in power, however, always has some superior qualities because of which others submit to it. This submission can be explicit and can have the character of a wholehearted concurrence. Or, as is far more frequently the case, it may have the character of tacit approval, without being openly expressed at all. It can also be involuntary, and yet quite real. This happens when one submits to a power to which neither an explicit nor an implicit assent can be freely given, and yet to which one gives a free hand in order not to endanger the unity of the social will. This is a form of "loyal opposition" that still gives assent, even if restrained by criticism, to the authority of the group in power.

The presupposition for this is that the critique of the group in power does not lead to the withdrawing of even this restrained assent, since that would be equivalent to revolution. In a revolution, the power structure is dissolved when the dominant group's capacity to prevail has been thrown into question. This question is decided in the power struggle.

Essential to every established power, therefore, is the consent of those who are subjected to it. If such consent ceases, power ceases, and the struggle to establish it on a new basis begins. In this struggle the group in power is still able, for a longer or a shorter time, to use force by employing its power apparatus. But so long as a revolutionary situation obtains, this is no longer the exercise of real power, but only an episode in the struggle for power. Power in the true sense implies a serene confidence in one's ability to prevail, while the exercise of force remains in the background as only a final possibility. A power that has to insert this background into the foreground, maintaining itself only through the exercise of force, has ceased to be power. It has become one of the groups fighting for power. Its capacity to prevail has been thrown into question; it can be renewed, but it can also be terminated. To be sure, a power can exercise force, and can even be established through force, if it subsequently gains social assent. A power can even maintain itself by force for a time when this assent has been withdrawn. But power is never based on force; it is always grounded in consent, whether expressed or unexpressed or, perhaps, fragmentary.

Such consent is given because those who assent to the exercise of power consider the way in which the unified will is executed to be just. *The exercise of power appears to be just when all members of a society can acknowledge that their own will is contained in the will of the whole.* It is not at all necessary that their will prevail without any restraint. The unified will can be perceived as quite just when the will of a particular group, including one's own, is coordinated with the will of other groups. The unified will as expressed by the leading group appears unjust only when it is perceived as being in flat contradiction to the will of a certain group. Such a group feels that it is not getting its just due. It must therefore withdraw its consent from the power structure; it must attempt to eliminate the dominant power as a power. But it can do this only by taking power itself. And in order to have its own power, it must demonstrate qualities that will be acknowledged by the other social groups, and for the sake of which the latter would be prepared to subject themselves to the new group, to yield it assent, even if limited assent. *The revolutionary group must be perceived by the people as the instrument of an over-arching justice. Only then does it have the chance to prevail in its struggle against the group in power.* If this is not the case, it can indeed gain control of the power apparatus by a *coup de main,* but it cannot establish a basis for true power.

It is not necessary that the assent of the other groups be explicit. But it is very necessary that strong and unremitting human energies be put at the disposal of this power, and that the opposing forces either give their silent consent, or else serve as a loyal opposition. If that does happen, again we have not power but a power struggle. From this it follows that in the power struggle, justice decides the issue in the final analysis—not an absolute, abstract justice, but a concrete justice that is perceived at a given time by a society and its particular groups as justice *for them.* In this sense, all power is based on justice.

It might seem that connecting the ideal of justice with the group in power in this manner amounts to a surrender of the ideal of justice to the powers of origin. The "ought" appears to be swallowed up by the "is," and the "Whither" by the "Whence." But this is not the case. Justice has an overarching character. It is, to be sure, bound to concrete social forces. But it does not therefore cease being a demand. This corresponds to the two elements exhibited in human being, as well as to the socialist principle: the "ought" is the fulfillment of the "is." *Justice is not an abstract ideal standing over existence; it is the fulfillment of primal being,* the fulfillment of that which was intended by the origin. Justice is not bound to the actual powers of origin and their ambiguity. Were this the case, justice would, in fact, be dissolved into mere being. It is bound to the true origin that it fulfills, but fulfills concretely. Therefore justice presses beyond every social situation, for every reality reflects the ambiguity of origin. It is the function of the prophetic movements of a particular period to expose this ambiguity and to fight for a more adequate justice. But this struggle can only be led by a group that can represent and realize the new justice. This is precisely the situation of the proletariat. The classless society is *its* justice, but, at the same time, it is justice per se, which must be counterposed to capitalism on capitalist soil. Because it is *its* justice, and insofar as it is, the proletariat must be the leading power in a society that subjects itself to this ideal of justire. *Socialism has no cause to pursue the utopia of a society without power, a notion that derives from the bourgeois principle and depends on the belief in natural harmony.* Rather, it must understand the power that it wins and defends as a realization of *this* justice for *this* time and in *this* social situation. So the problem of power proves to be the problem of a concrete justice.[20]

The structure of the state rests on this relationship between power and justice. Necessary as it is to reject the bourgeois state as a class state, and inadequate as the prebourgeois structures of the state are as a standard for today, it would be a mistake to deduce the concept of the state from the misuse of its power in a class state, and hence to expect its dissolution into various social functions in the classless society. Unified social functions occur only when there is a unified consensus, and that cannot be attained by natural harmony, but only through the exercise of power. Thus the key question is this: How can the power structure be designed to allow the greatest possible opportunity for true power, i.e., just power, to be actualized?

Democracy believes it possible to form a social structure without authoritative power groups. Power belongs to all, and is transferred to those chosen by the majority. But the concept of the majority contains a dialectical element that transcends democracy, namely in the manner in which the majority is constituted. It is possible that democracy, though present in form, is in fact made inoperative by the ruling group. This is exactly the situation in a state based on a class system. From this point of view, the demand for a "dictatorship of the proletariat" can be understood as a call for the abolition of a pseudodemocracy that conceals bourgeois class domination. The experience of bourgeois democracy thus confirms the point that there is no social structure without a power group. The difference between democracy and the prebourgeois forms of the state is only this: in a democracy, power groups, even though limited in their scope, dominate without being accountable, while in predemocratic circumstances they are accountable, but therefore unlimited. For socialism this implies a demand that socialism's leading groups, as power groups, be made accountable, yet also subject to democratic controls. Accountability and restraint must be combined.

The democratic principle is in the first instance a *corrective*. It cannot be decided in a democratic way which group is called to exercise social power. That is decided behind the scenes by the real significance a group has in society. But it is certainly possible and necessary to put the existing powers under the scrutiny of the demand of justice, not in an abstract way, but in such a way that all groups are given the possibility of asserting their own demand for justice. But this is possible only through democracy. Therein lies its justification and its permanent significance, which will endure even after the destruction of the bourgeois principle. Therein lies its prophetic element. Therefore, every movement that seeks a simple return to origin must oppose democracy. This is made easier for political thought tied to the origin by democracy's attempt to make itself a constitutive principle. But this it cannot be. It cannot create anything, for the powers of origin are required for every creative act. But it can give creativity a direction. It can balance, criticize, reveal injustice, and contest the misuse of power. *The construction of the socialist state must be carried out within the tension between the powers of origin that support the structure of society and the democratic corrective that subjects it to the demand of justice.*

These thoughts concerning power and the state have important consequences for socialist theory and praxis. Socialist theory, insofar as it involves an interpretation of history, must guard against projecting the current intrabourgeois situation back into the past. Older forms of domination should not be interpreted as instances of class domination, especially if class consciousness is considered a distinguishing characteristic of a class. *The prebourgeois forms of domination should not be measured by an abstract, natural-law ideal of justice, but rather by the ideal of justice on which they themselves were based.* Even the lower classes (except in the rare cases of sectarian-utopian movements) have never measured the rule of the power-bearing groups by anything other than the ideal that these groups themselves defended, e.g., the patriarchal ideal of justice. Thus the demands of the peasants in the German Peasants' War did not go beyond what was meaningful in terms of the feudal system itself. They represented a struggle against injustices that had arisen in the context of this system, contrary to its own original intention. It was only under the aegis of the bourgeois principle that a new demand for justice was voiced, one based on an absolute natural law.[21] The proletariat, in correspondence with its situation, adopted the natural law ideal of the bourgeoisie, and agressively struggled to realize it. In this struggle the proletariat not only meets the opposition of those who support injustice, who represent bourgeois class domination; it also is opposed by other ideals of justice represented by prebourgeois groups. At the same time, it comes to the realization that absolute natural law is nowhere taken seriously as a basis, indeed, that it cannot be implemented successfully within the proletarian movement itself. Thus socialism is obliged to formulate a new ideal of justice, one that is neither bourgeois nor prebourgeois. In the accomplishment of this, a genuine encounter with the prebourgeois revolutionized classes can be of essential significance.

It is important for the theory of revolution that the attainment of power in society always presupposes the possession of certain qualities that persuade other groups to subject themselves to the group holding power. The development of such qualities is thus just as necessary for the revolutionary process as is the seizure of the power apparatus. This takes place invisibly, slowly, and in constant struggle within the group itself and in its encounter with other groups. It was the distinctive insight of reformism that it acknowledged this process as having revolutionary significance. Its mistake was that it neglected to make preparation for the other process, namely the assumption of power. Consequently, when extensive power fell into the lap of the Social Democratic party, it proved unable to exercise and consolidate it in a manner that would have reflected the inner power of the socialist movement.

The evaluation of democracy as corrective, rather than constitutive, for the structuring of society implies that socialism must restrict democracy on the one hand, while radicalizing it on the other. It must restrict democracy in those areas of life that demand daily, concrete, well-informed decision making, areas that presuppose a capacity for the independent exercise of power. Democracy is not intended to be a machine that operates continuously. It should assume its function only when fundamental decisions are being made, and above all, when the exercise of power by the dominant groups demands a corrective in the name of justice. We can say nothing here concerning the legal forms in which this concept of *democracy as being more corrective than constitutive* may be embodied. It should be clear, in any case, that these forms have nothing to do with the bourgeois and feudal attempts at reaction in an antidemocratic, authoritarian sense. Socialism can rebuff such efforts only to the extent that it frees itself from its association with the bourgeois principle, and does justice to both elements of its own principle, the origin and the goal.

4. Symbol and Concept in the Development of Culture

The inner conflict of the socialist idea of culture is resolvable as soon as socialism draws the consequences of its principle, i.e., when it grasps the significance of the origin for its attitude toward religion and science, education and culture. But if that happens, its policy toward culture must undergo thorough and vigorous self-criticism.

This applies, first of all, to its attitude toward religion and the churches. Socialism is quite justified in continuing to attempt to limit the political influence of the churches as they are presently structured, but it is quite unjustified in its privatization of religion along the lines of the liberal idea of tolerance. Socialism has a twofold task vis-à-vis the churches. *First of all, it must represent the socialist idea within their midst.*[22] It must bring to expression in the churches the prophetic element that is alive in socialism, and on which all religious groups in the Judeo-Christian tradition depend. Socialism has to demonstrate that they have limited and even betrayed the attitude of expectation which they themselves once possessed, in favor of the powers related to the myth of origin. *Socialism has to strengthen the prophetic as opposed to the priestly element in the churches.* "Religious socialism" has attempted to do just this. It has achieved an important initial success in Protestantism, while remaining unsuccessful thus far in Catholicism. The domination of the priesthood in Catholicism explains this situation. What is surprising is that quite the opposite is true so far as tactics are concerned, where we find that socialism moves toward an alliance, not with the Catholic church as such, but with the Center party,* a tactic that brings it into opposition to the overwhelming majority of Protestants, and this in spite of the fact that its principle stands so much closer to the Protestant principle than to the Catholic. Protestantism has the possibility of taking the socialist principle into itself under the aspect of the New Testament concept of the *kairos*.[23] Catholicism does not appear to have this possibility, at least not at present.

Such an intraconfessional, and especially intra-Protestant, project of socialism could have as its consequence the emergence, out of an alliance of Christianity and socialism, of an historical form

* *Zentrumspartei*, a political party founded in 1870 to represent Roman Catholic viewpoints and interests. Played a major role in national and regional government during the Weimar Republic, in coalition with the Social Democrats.—TRANS.

of Christianity in which the opposition between the religious and the profane, the churchly and the secular, no longer has any meaning.[24]

For this to occur, however, it is necessary, further, that socialism reexamine itself and its beliefs. It has left this function until now to the *freethinker movement*. At present, however, it appears to be distancing itself from this movement. And properly so, for the freethinker movement is a purely bourgeois phenomenon. It is an attempt to restore the religious bond of origin by the use of means which serve to undercut this bond. This explains the religious powerlessness of this movement, in comparison with which even the most myth-bound churches show themselves to be religiously powerful.[25] This experience should convince socialism of the significance of the religious tradition. *It is only out of the tensions of the religious tradition that new religious life has ever sprung.* That is the significance of the churches' preservation of the religious powers of origin in an age that is characterized by autonomy and objectification. *The socialist principle makes it possible for socialism to understand itself in terms of its own roots, and that means, religiously, and on the basis of its own prophetic element to take up a relationship again with the prophetic elements in the history of Western religion.*

Such a change is all the more necessary since the socialist belief in science has been shaken on all sides. *Science as a substitute for religion is found only among those who have never participated in the actual life of science,* and for whom, consequently, the preliminary results of scientific research could assume a dogmatic status. Scientific dogmatism is found abundantly among the socialist proletariat, ostensibly functioning as scientific results, but in reality functioning as articles of faith around which socialist belief itself developed. This carries with it the danger that continuing scientific work and the spread of new scientific views will shake not only the conceptual form but also the symbolic content of socialism, and thereby socialist belief as such. It is of greatest importance that the socialist leadership inform itself as soon as possible concerning this situation, and that it take the initiative to disengage the masses from their threatened—and rightly threatened—faith in science, and to find a way to express the socialist faith in a new, symbolically powerful form. Such symbols will probably not differ completely from the traditional symbolic language of religion. At the same time, they must be related to secular language insofar as the latter has achieved a symbolically powerful vocabulary. *The future symbolic language can be developed only through a combination of religious and secular symbolism.* Therefore, the socialist movement's task of seeking out new symbols must be pursued in close association with the churches' equally urgent task of translating the religiously symbolic language of the past into the secular consciousness of the present.[26] From this follows the point of view toward education that the socialist principle implies. The concept of the "secular"— a polemical concept directed against a rigid and politically powerful ecclesiasticism—must be overcome in the interest of a prophetic, socialist faith. Only thus can a foundation be created for socialist pedagogy. The protest of numerous socialist mothers against a nonreligious education and the secular school rests not on an unenlightened and reactionary consciousness, but on their instinctive wisdom concerning the supportive powers of origin. Many socialist parents find themselves, consequently, in a position of severe conflict between the party's demand for secular schools, which they must reject, and the traditional church schools, hostile to socialism, which they cannot accept either. Usually they choose the latter as the lesser of two evils. This pedagogical conflict can only be resolved in a school in which origin and prophetic demand stand in living tension and in practical balance.

Socialist pedagogy will be forced to move in this direction as soon as its faith in the symbolic power of scientific concepts has been given up. Of course, that step is rendered difficult by the romantic effort to cloak science in a veil of slogans, over against which the demand for clear and pure analysis remains correct under all conditions. But socialism does not need to let its opponents prescribe for it the law of its own thought.[27] *It can totally reject this obfuscation of the rational methods of knowledge and still acknowledge the limits of the significance of knowledge for life.* The actual socialist movement, as well as the political events in the opposing camp, are constant evidence of the power of the symbolic, whether expressed in persons, actions, or ensigns. Symbols have proven superior to concepts and arguments among all groups, including the proletariat. This, too, is not due to a defective development of consciousness, but to a legitimate feeling for the inability of concepts to contain the totality of a living entity, and to an awareness of the ability of the symbolic to express the power of being. Symbols, however, belong to the realm of the origin. To the extent that symbols possessing immediate power are available, socialist education has the possibility of achieving that which is the essence of education: induction into the leading groups of a society.

Education is a matter of induction. But induction presupposes that there is something to be inducted into. Wherever the bourgeois principle is operative, all powers and forms related to the origin are dissolved. Consequently, in correspondence with the rational scientific approach, induction can only mean induction into that abstraction, "human possibility in general," which is to say that there cannot really be any induction at all. Thus we have education as merely the communication of information, cut off from the real situation of the pupils. That is still tolerable if we are speaking of a thoroughly humanistic education that introduces the student to the highest forms of humanistic culture. It is intolerable when only small fragments and byproducts of humanism can be transmitted. Therefore the socialist idea of education must abandon its pseudohumanistic bourgeois basis and rather aim at induction into concrete groups and their supporting symbols. To be specific, it must provide an induction into the socialist movement, its structures and its symbolism. This can conflict with the national educational program as a whole only insofar as the latter expresses (and at the same time obscures) the domination of the bourgeois classes. Insofar as this is in fact the case, socialism must wage the same kind of passionate struggle against the government's concept of education that the churches, in an earlier period, were prepared to wage when public education began to undermine the churches' substance.[28]

With these observations, the question of a *socialist ideal of education* has been already answered. Only those intellectual forms through which the socialist movement can interpret itself, its meaning, its past, and its possible future have educational significance in the context of a socialism open to the dimension of the origin. This is true with regard to the universal as well as the particular import of socialism. It does not imply any restriction of the materials employed by the humanistic idea of education. But it does mean that these materials are understood and utilized educationally from a concrete standpoint and in terms of a specific line of action. Abstract education through that which is "human in general" (actually, human in a bourgeois sense) is overcome through an intentionally concrete concept of education, namely, that of socialism.[29]

To the extent to which socialism fosters the development of the powers of origin, its own powers of cultural creativity will also come alive. The limits of a proletarian culture can only be overcome by a universal socialist culture. The far-ranging objectification to which the proletariat has been subject by virtue of class domination must be overcome if there is to be a socialist culture. For all spiritual productivity, all culture, lives out of the powers of origin, even when its intention is to break the powers of origin and to subject them to the unconditional demand. The symbolic does not displace the conceptual. A concept can itself become a symbol; this has happened very frequently in the past. And a symbol can embody and express a certain concept of reality. Symbols do not create a heteronomy. They need not do so, and so far as socialism is concerned, must not do so. This statement is directed equally against the new mythology that Fascism is trying to create, so as to enlist its help in warding off rational criticism, and also against the dogmatizing of scientific concepts that, given the status of symbols, function heteronomously as in the case of Bolshevism. Socialism is oriented toward autonomy. But it is as true of intellectual autonomy and political democracy as of the bourgeois principle in general that it is corrective, not constitutive. If it is made constitutive, there results the tragedy of an autonomy that produces its own dissolution, as exemplified in

Greek antiquity. Autonomy, while putting all of its own assertions into radical question, itself undergoes dissolution as soon as the powers of origin from which positive answers can arise have disappeared. *Reason can neither ground nor construct anything by itself. But it is the judge of every act of grounding and every construct.* Nothing is to be shielded from it; even the holiest symbol is subject to its criticism. Whether this criticism leads to the destruction or the renewal of the symbol depends not on reason, but on the power of the symbol to disclose to reason levels of being that had been hidden from it. One cannot defend symbols by putting up windbreakers to shelter them from rational criticism. Either the symbols protect themselves or they prove to be powerless, and then it is time to abandon them. For every symbol participates in the ambiguity of origin, and is subject, therefore, to prophetic and rational criticism. Culture cannot be "saved" by muzzling critical reason. It is saved only when the reality in which it is rooted proves itself to be the stronger—not by repressing reason, but by revealing to reason the inner infinity of being, and at the same time, by offering it support and structure.

5. *Eros and Purpose in the Life of the Community*

The inner conflict in the socialist idea of community has led to serious difficulties. The dissolution of all communal bonds in proletarian existence is determinative for the proletarian consciousness, and deprives it of the capacity to appreciate the communal bonds that still do exist. The reactionary forces, which have taken possession of the family and the national community, compel the proletariat to assume a permanent posture of protest, a posture that contradicts its own desire for a new community.

As to the *idea of the nation*, what can be said on the basis of the socialist principle is the following. Undeterred by ideological talk of a national community, socialism must decisively and courageously unveil the bourgeois perversion of the national idea, revealing that the spirit of patriotism is being used to justify and defend class domination at home and economic imperialism abroad. Even at present a considerable portion, if not the greatest portion, of the self-destructive nationalism of the European peoples can be traced back to such sources. *But it is true here, too, that only what once had a genuine use can be misused.* The idea of the nation cannot be destroyed by pointing to its perversion. The idea of the nation has energies deriving from the origin, and therefore has a claim to fulfillment—meaning not uncritical support, but also not destruction. Soil, blood, tradition, the social group—all the powers of origin are combined in the nation. The prophetic tradition thus relates to a people neither in such a way as to confirm it in its immediate self-awareness (as the "false prophets" do), nor to dissolve it for the sake of an immediate transition to a universal humanity (as bourgeois cosmopolitanism does). It seeks rather at once to judge and to support the nation. *The prophetic is always addressed to all humanity, but it always proceeds from amongst a people,* exhibiting thereby the unity of origin and goal that is typical of it.

Partly against its own will, and therefore with some inner uncertainty, socialism has been forced by history to this attitude toward nationhood. *Socialism must enter into relationship with a people if it is to win acceptance among them.* For the sake of its own calling, socialism must affirm the nation, and with this, the tensions among the nations. But at the same time, it must destroy any claim that a particular people is directly identified with the absolute. Over against the tensions among the nations, it must set the overarching concept of humanity as a goal. Concretely, this means that in accordance with the prophetic character of its expectation, socialism must place the people to which it belongs, and which it seeks to lead toward socialism, under the unconditional demand of justice, both at home and abroad. It must employ all the power that it has at its command to prevent the violation of the demands of justice, either at home or abroad, in the name of an expansion of national power. It must support all tendencies that can aid the development of an overarching sense of justice, even if for the time being this is misused by imperialistic power groups such as the League of Nations. *Socialism must affirm the nation more profoundly than nationalism can.* Nationalism, as a movement expressing the myth of origin, drives a nation necessarily into the cycle of birth, development, and death. Nationalism can provide the nation with an empire, but it cannot so relate it to the course of history as to free it from the cycle of birth and death. Socialism performs a service for Christian peoples which the churches have relinquished, if not formally, then actually, among many of its groups and leaders: *It frees the nations from the law of death by subjecting them to the prophetic demand.* Therefore prophetism alone truly serves the nation. It is the legitimate representative of the idea of the nation. And what is true for prophetism is also true for socialism.

In Germany, socialism has worked for the emancipation of women, and theoretically, at least, has achieved their virtual equality before the law. In so doing, it has carried out the legacy of liberalism. At the same time, it has sought to do justice to economic needs. And yet, for the most part, women have utilized their political emancipation to work against socialism. It is especially with the help of women that political romanticism is seeking to deprive women of their rights. That has proved possible because women, though emancipated in the liberal sense, did not immediately attain to a higher level of fulfillment, as was posited by the bourgeois belief in harmony. Instead they fell first into a situation analogous to the class situation into which the liberated proletarian had been thrown. Generally speaking, the economic power of women in free competition turns out to be less than that of men, while the psychological power of women is more deeply opposed to the mechanical forms of a rationalized economic system.[30] *The powers of origin possessed by woman by virtue of her resonance with eros and motherhood cannot easily be incorporated into the extremely onesided, male-oriented rationalistic system.* Just as it supported the proletarian movement over against class rule, so socialism should support the women's movement that sets itself against this tendency of the bourgeois principle. It should be obvious that such a movement has nothing to do with the rather ridiculous attempts of political romanticism to force the new type of woman back into a particular spiritual, physical, sexual, and legal mold. Socialism cannot possibly tolerate the restoration of male partriarchalism. Above all, socialism must totally reject every attempt to reintroduce the inhumanity of the double standard in morality, the ostracism of illegitimate children, and unrestricted procreation. Socialism can ward off this dangerous reaction only by relating woman's powers of origin to the socialist struggle, precisely at those places where a general awakening of the powers of origin for the sake of the socialist principle is needed, above all in cultural and community life.

These are only examples. One of the most pressing tasks which socialist theory and praxis have to pursue in the next few years is the creation of a full-fledged *socialist social ethic.*

6. Nature and Planning in the Economic Order

The antinomy in the socialist idea of economics stemmed from socialism's having to align itself with liberalism over against the restraints on economic rationality, while at the same time affirming the necessity of central planning in view of the consequences of capitalism. The question was raised as to who is to be in charge of this central planning, and how a locus of pure economic reason might be found.

This question finds its basic answer in the theory of social structure that we have developed. There is no such thing as a point of pure reason in economics, any more than there is any such thing as abstract democracy or abstract justice. Economics, too, is the expression of a concrete social situation, decisively influenced by certain groups. What shall be produced? At what expenditure of psychological and social power? To what extent, and in what form, is technological progress to be permitted? What level of international economic interdependence is necessary or tolerable? None of these is a question of pure economic reason. The answers given to them reflect concrete human existence, the powers of origin and the goals of leading social groups. Only on this basis and in this framework is pure economic theory valid, and even then it has its limits.

A consistent liberal theory does not acknowledge such limits. It subordinates the life-process itself to economic rationalization, just as radical democracy seeks to turn the state into a function of an abstract idea of justice. *But only concrete justice and a concrete form of economic life express reality. In them, the dominant productive forces of a society at a given time come to expression.* As a polemic against absolutism, liberalism was for the bourgeoisie a real expression of its productive powers. It was the appropriate concept for the economically and politically proficient group at that time. But liberalism was curtailed by this very group as soon as the basic hindrances to the development of its productive forces had been removed and the question became one of constructive economic development within individual countries.

Liberalism discovered that the actual economic process does obey certain laws, but that even so, it is as impossible to derive the real substance of economics from these laws as it is impossible to derive the spatial-temporal world from the laws of physics. In nature as well as economics, the structure is conditioned by the origin. What rational analysis has made clear is the regularity of economic laws that all structures must reflect, and which in the economic sphere do lend themselves to technical and rational management. Socialism's primary challenge is, in the first place, to know and to affirm the real dynamics of socialist economics and the concrete economic purpose contained therein. It is the economic purpose of the group supporting socialism, above all, of the proletariat, that determines the direction and the form of socialist economics.

This can be elucidated in four respects: with regard to the question of needs; the attitude toward technological progress; the attitude toward work; and the relation of an origin-related economics to international economics. Only when an economic aim has been thought through in terms of these four dimensions can the question of its technical realization be dealt with.

In bourgeois society, economic demand is based on a peculiar mixture of traditional needs and others that are created only through the possibility of their being satisfied. But since even traditional needs are invariant only in content (food, clothing, shelter), while their form is mutable, there arises from both sides a strong tendency toward the alteration and increase of needs which makes anticipation of economic demands very difficult. The natural determination that occurs through the market mechanism, in view of the complexity of the productive enterprise, usually takes place too late for the strength and direction of the demand to play a role in the shaping of production. This accounts in part for the wrong investments that lead to continual disruptions, but nevertheless are inherent in a free market economy. In the socialist scheme of things, this unlimited possibility of stimulating new needs is excluded, for the following reasons. First, because decisions concerning the capital to be invested in creating the means of production are determined by a central planning unit according to the measure of *actually existing needs* and the urgency they have in the social consciousness. Second, because the equalization of incomes is bound to have as a consequence a significant *standardization of needs*. Third, because of the increasing assimilation into socialism of origin-related groups, *need traditions* will be developed that make it possible to determine the direction of needs. People who succumb to the temptation of the infinite possibilities for need-satisfaction tend to fall into complete insecurity, aimlessness, and indeterminateness in the defining and valuation of these needs. Such persons have become slaves to their own possibilities. Through socialism, they will learn to subordinate possibility to actuality. *Possible needs will not create actual needs; rather, actual needs will make use of the possibilities for satisfaction made available by technology.* A "dictatorship of needs" thus is unnecessary. What is required is only the determination of actual needs, and, in the case of conflict among them, arbitration by the central authority. In the case of equally strong demands, the central authority will decide in favor of the need having priority in terms of social value.

The same considerations will determine socialism's attitude toward technological progress. Technological progress as such is an expression of the human ability to move beyond all that is given toward that which is projected. Ever since the projection of the utopias of the Renaissance and the discoveries of mathematical natural science, Western civilization has been systemati-

cally transforming the possibility of technological progress—
which in itself is infinite—into reality. This is the world historical
achievement of bourgeois society. It has led the masses out of
mute bondage and, frequently, from subhuman subjection to
nature into a domination of nature. But it has done this in a
manner that has proved increasingly disastrous, and has led to
strong antitechnological reactions. *The misuse of technological
possibilities in capitalist society awakened the forces of antitechnological romanticism.*[31] Competition forced the individual entrepreneur or group of entrepreneurs to improve the technical
means of production to such an extent and to rationalize the
methods of production so broadly that on one hand, a large labor
force was permanently excluded from employment, while on the
other hand, the market was not able to absorb the products that
could be produced by the existing apparatus, indeed, not even a
fraction of what had to be produced under the pressure to make
use of the invested capital. Technological rationalization within
the framework of free competition thus proved to be the chief
factor in the economic crisis. It led to the absurd result that with
the ever-increasing, indeed nearly limitless, possibilities of production, an immense impoverishment occurred which to an un-
precedented extent made it impossible to satisfy basic needs.

The lesson for socialism is that rationalizaion through central
planning must take into account the capacity of the market for
economic consumption, while the false technological rationalization resulting from competition is made impossible. There need
be no fear that this will interfere with such technological progress
as is economically possible; in any case, no more so than in the
capitalistic system itself, which constantly sees socially valuable
inventions suppressed and rejected for the sake of profit—quite
apart from the periodic stoppage of technological progress during
an economic crisis. Technological progress is another of those
consequences of the bourgeois principle that in themselves are
abstract and can only be actualized meaningfully by incorpora-
tion into the actual possibilities of the life-process. Technological
progress in itself has infinite possibilities. Some of them will be
achieved at a particular time, but progress itself cannot determine

which ones, and it must not be left to capitalistic caprice. The social will must make the decision, as it is expressed in an interaction between the traditional needs as determined by the market and the decisions of the central authority.

Just as the laws of the marketplace and technological possibility must be related to the life-process of individuals and of society, so too must work. In the socialist society, work must no longer be permitted to dominate as it does today in the form of a limitless demand for work, on the one hand, alternating, on the other hand, with a total suspension of it, a situation that is the inescapable result of the natural laws of a free economy.

There is, of course, a natural necessity to work that is derived from the origin, and which is in no way to be abandoned. Some kinds of work are less fully satisfying than other kinds; this also cannot be changed. And the element of fatiguing drudgery that is connected with even the most satisfying work ought not be obscured by a romantic and ideological glorification of work. It is completely ridiculous to say that work is religion. Socialist belief deals with work and its burdens as it deals with all natural phenomena. It does not make of it, as some theologians are wont to do, a justification for the senseless work-slavery that capitalistic competition imposes on all who are caught up in it. Nor does socialism romanticize the precapitalist, pretechnological forms of work. It affirms the use of the machine in order to liberate human beings from all merely *mechanical functions*. It seeks to fulfill the meaning of work through a structure in which the purpose, form, and relationships of work are so constituted that work serves people and does not destroy them.

The *purpose of work* in a socialist society is the satisfaction of those needs that can be satisfied through a well-organized, centrally controlled economy without market fluctuations and economic crises even when the goad of unlimited possibilities for profit and the lash of the threat of economic disaster are absent. It is possible that this way may be less productive. But it is also possible that the abolition of all the disruptions and production stoppages that stem from economic crises and imperialist wars would compensate abundantly for any shortfall. After the experience of the last war and the postwar crisis, this seems quite probable. But even if there were a lowering of productivity, that would be a small price to pay for the subordination of the economy to human need.

The *form of work* in the socialist economy is to be restructured by making accessible to the worker an understanding of the total process of production in which he is involved. The pernicious effects of specialization will thereby be lessened. Above all, a centrally controlled production process makes it possible to transfer the purely mechanical elements to the work of the machine, since the viewpoint of private enterprise that sees labor as often being cheaper than machinery would in principle be eliminated. A form of work ameliorated in this way could not indeed make *the meaning of life and the meaning of work* coincide. That is never possible. But it could reduce the intolerable tension that exists between them at the present time.

Finally, as to *work relationships*, the socialist order liberates workers from having to work for someone else's profit; it frees them to work for the community to which they themselves belong as contributing members. To the employer, it provides freedom from the pressure of unrestricted competitive struggle and an integration into the common productive enterprise (perhaps by assuming a managerial role). This means *the replacement of profits won by economic rivalry with prizes won, as it were, in an athletic contest.* For both groups socialism means the end of class opposition, with its poisoning of the total life of work through the unavoidable conflict of interest in a merely forced unification of the work process.[32]

The socialist principle also contains the possibility of solving the problem, which is particularly acute today, of the relation between the national and the world economy. *An autarky of the national economy implies, in keeping with the myth of origin, tying production to a limited space, for the sake of the absolute sovereignty of this space.* But no one space is sovereign. International trade and exchange, of its own force, prevails over the economic independence of places bound to the origin. It is a pathbreaker for the trans-spatial unity of humankind, for a common orientation to the forward movement of time. Hence the prophetic position affirms the international horizon, also with regard to economic exchange. Prophetism protects the "alien" in the name of the same unconditional demand that compatriots and foreigners, one's own and other peoples, all confront: the demand of justice.

But exchange is only possible on a certain basis, a ground on which to stand, an economic tradition. If the movement towards autarky has any significance, it can only reside in the creation of a more secure basis for international economic exchange, and in the prevention of an absorption into the international economy. For the turn towards time does not mean the abrogation of space. Space, however, has reality only in specific spaces and their particular powers of origin. These must be affirmed, even if from a purely economic point of view they might be unnecessary for world production. Protecting them must involve at the same time, of course, changing their structures to correspond with the significance they can actually have in a rational, worldwide productive enterprise, rather than maintaining absolute structures at the price of economic sacrifices that must be borne by the national and international economy. For the goal of socialist economics is the *unification of world economic space* and the rational utilization of the earth's virtually unlimited productive possibilities in the service of humanity as a whole and of all its constituent groups.

One must now ask how this is possible from the standpoint of the laws of economics. The answer is provided by socialist economics; indeed socialist economics has already given the answer, in connection with the actual developmental trends of the present period. *Positions of economic power held by private enterprise must be placed in the hands of society as a whole,* and that means in the hands of the leading groups in the social structure. These positions of power include *the landed estates, heavy industry, major manufacturing concerns, banking, and foreign trade.* This having been done, the whole process of production can be managed according to the socialist principle. On this basis, the problem of economic rationalization can be solved, so that the destructive effects of technological rationalization are abolished and are turned into the opposite. In this way it becomes possible *to preserve the free market*, which serves as a register of needs and as the regulator of the direction of production and the establishment of prices—all, to be sure, within the perimeters of central planning. This means, further, that in those forms of production that do not constitute positions of authority in society, a free economy can be preserved, and thus the bureaucratization of the whole economy can be avoided. Where bureaucracy is unavoidable, it has long since appeared as part of the development of advanced capitalism.

Thus the basic thrust of the socialist principle is demonstrated also in the question of socialist economics: the shattering of the bourgeois belief in harmony, and the uniting of nature and planning in the structuring of the economy.[33]

Conclusion: The Future of Socialism

The socialist principle is able to solve the antinomies of socialism. It is superior not only to the bourgeois principle, but to the romantic principle as well. It alone has the power to create a future for Western civilization. The collapse of the bourgeois principle is becoming increasingly obvious with every crisis of capitalism. All forms of belief in harmony are dying out. Reality has refuted this belief. The conservative form of political romanticism offers no new principle adequate to the social situation. It can gain power for a limited time through military means, but in the long run it cannot succeed. The revolutionary form of political romanticism has only two options; either to revert to the conservative form (and the more decisive its victory, the more likely this is), or to become socialist. The latter would involve a casting off of the specifically romantic elements and an integration of the powers related to the myth of origin within the prophetic movement of the present day, namely, socialism. The unqualified superiority of the socialist principle is, of course, no guarantee of victory for the socialist movement. There is also, as Marx saw, another possibility: chaos. If, in the encounter between the bourgeoisie and political romanticism, the bourgeois principle should once again gain a complete victory, the increasingly severe crises would make chaos virtually inevitable. If on the other hand political romanticism and, with it, militant nationalism proves victorious, a self-annihilating struggle of the European peoples is inevitable. *The salvation of European society from a return to barbarism lies in the hands of socialism.* Only socialism can make certain that the unlimited possibilities for technical domination of the world that have been created in the bourgeois period will remain under human control and will be employed for the service of humanity. Only socialism can prevent these possibilities from becoming the means of their own self-destruction and that of the very society that wrested them from nature.

It is the industrial proletariat that is called, in the first instance, to be the bearer of socialism. *The proletariat still holds the key position in the contemporary social situation, because it stands most clearly on the negative side.* It will hold this position as long as bourgeois capitalism lasts. When compared to the reality of the split between the classes, every other fact about society becomes less important. Every social group is drawn into the structure of confrontation that is inherent in the liberal bourgeois system. The proletariat by its very existence is thrust towards socialism. It cannot do otherwise as long as, and insofar as, it is the proletariat.

At the same time, the notion that the victory of socialism can be won by the proletariat alone must be contested. Certainly it cannot be done without the proletariat, for the proletariat is the necessary condition for any realization of socialism. But it is, at least for the present, not the sufficient condition. Precisely the situation that drives the proletariat into socialism also creates the limits of the proletariat's ability to achieve socialism by itself. *In the present situation, it is dependent on the origin-related powers. Without them, socialism cannot win victory at this time.* The future of socialism, and the fate of Germany and the European peoples as well, depend on this alliance. Whether it will in fact be realized, or whether the proletarianization of almost all strata of society will make it unnecessary, will be decided by the inner

development of capitalist society. It will be decided in the inseparable connection between economic laws and the human beings
through whom they are effected. Since laws do have a role of
codetermination, the future of the West is not wholly unclear; but
since they exercise this codetermination only through human action, no unequivocal calculation is possible. Since human action
shares in the determination, the future of Western civilization can
be either socialism or barbarism. But since human action has this
freedom only within the framework of economic and social laws,
there is basically no third possibility beyond these two.

The fact that many groups related to the myth of origin are
being revolutionized by the current economic crisis and that they
have stood up in opposition to capitalism and thus have broken
up the bourgeois political center, is the strongest positive indica-
tion for a socialist victory. On the other hand, the fact that they
are doing so under the aegis of a blatant nationalism and with the
spiritual and material support of certain bourgeois groups en-
gaged in the class struggle is the greatest danger to socialism.
Socialism is being forced by external pressure into a posture of
defensiveness, surrendering its revolutionary energies to political
romanticism. Furthermore, in its resistance to political romanticism, it is permitting itself to be forced back upon its bourgeois
elements. But it is only by rejecting these elements that it can be
victorious, since it is they that lead it into the inner conflict that
threatens its destruction. Socialism can be victorious only in reli-
ance on its own principle, in which powers of origin and prophetic expectation are combined. But expectation must play the
major role. Only through expectation is human existence raised to
the level of true humanity. Only under its leadership can human
being and human society find their fulfillment. The hegemony of
the myth of origin means the domination of violence and death.
*Only expectation can triumph over the death now threatening
Western civilization through the resurgence of the myth of origin.
And expectation is the symbol of socialism.*

Notes

Foreword

1. Cf. Hendrik [Henri] de Man, *Sozialismus und Nationalfaszismus* (Potsdam, 1931); Günter Keiser, "Der Nationalsozialismus, eine reaktionäre Revolution," *Neue Blätter fur den Sozialismus*, no. 6, 1931, pp. 270 ff.; further the whole of issue no. 4, 1931.

2. This kind of attitude is encountered above all among intellectuals on the fringe of Communism who without discussion will condemn an opposing idea as "bourgeois ideology," but who have never considered whether they themselves are not caught in an ideology—or in a *ressentiment*.

3. Particularly, *Zur Psychologie des Sozialismus*, 2nd ed. (Jena, 1927) [Engl. trans. by Eden and Cedar Paul, *The Psychology of Socialism* (New York: Holt, 1928)] and *Der Kampf um die Arbeitsfreude* (Jena, 1927) [Engl. trans. by Eden and Cedar Paul, *Joy in Work* (New York: Holt, 1929)] as well as his address in the volume *Sozialismus aus dem Glauben* (Zürich and Leipzig, 1929).

4. The "real" Marx is Marx in the context of his development, hence the unity of the younger and the older Marx. Only if the one is interpreted by the other is a true understanding of Marx possible. See below.

5. Cf. below, chap. 5, sec. 1, "The Powers of Origin in the Proletarian Movement."

6. Religious socialism is represented by the "Bund der religiösen Sozialisten Deutschlands" with its magazine *Zeitschrift für Religion und Sozialismus*, edited by Georg Wünsch, as well as by the "Bund der religiösen Sozialisten Österreichs," with its magazine *Menschheitskämpfer*, ed. Otto Bauer. The *Blätter für religiösen Sozialismus* was edited by Carl Mennicke and appeared in the years 1920–1927. The *Neue Blätter für den Sozialismus* has appeared since 1930, ed. Eduard Heimann, August Rathmann, and Paul Tillich.

Introduction: The Two Roots of Political Thought

1. I suggest to readers who find abstract philosophical thinking difficult that they omit the Introduction and begin with the exposition of political romanticism. The chapter on the problems of Marxism, with its difficult theoretical arguments, may also be omitted without seriously affecting one's understanding of the whole.

2. I refer especially to the events of 1932, particularly those of July 20 (the coup against Prussia).*

3. The distrust of anthropology shown by many Marxist theoreticians has its historical basis in Marx's turn away from Feuerbach. Against the Feuerbachian picture of "humanity in general" Marx places actual human beings, determined by class and society. But even these class determined human beings are still human, that is, entities that can have a history, that can live in society, that can be split into classes, that fall into "dehumanization" and "objectification," and that can struggle for a social order in which their destiny, a "real humanism," is fulfilled. This, however, presupposes structures that must be investigated for the light they shed on social movements, just as, conversely, the notion of human nature stands in the closest possible connection with the concrete social situation. What is said in the text is to be interpreted in the sense of this *reciprocal illumination of human being and social situation.* (Cf. also below, note 7.)

4. Cf. the section "The Problem of Historical Materialism," below, chap. 6, sec. 1.

5. The ambiguity of the origin is denied by a vitalistic philosophy such as Klages has developed in his great work, *Der Geist als Widersacher der Seele* [Leipzig, 1929, and subsequent editions]. The political effects of this philosophy compel socialism to challenge it. (See below, pp. 39 f.)

6. The "formal" establishment of justice as a *demand* is unavoidable if its unconditionality is not to be impugned. Hence Kantian "formalism," which remains valid even if justice as an *ideal* receives its content from a concrete situation, for example, the proletarian situation.

7. One could derive from this train of thought the methodological conclusion that it would be better to rest content with the historical realities and desist from any effort to deal with their roots. The latter, some would maintain, are unknowable and without reality; there are no independent, primal elements of human being apart from historical reality; human beings are what they are in their social situation at any

* A reference to the ouster by Chancellor Franz von Papen of the socialist regime in Prussia, an unconstitutional act but one that the Social Democrats proved unable to resist.—TRANS.

given time, and nothing more. But this chain of reasoning becomes self-contradictory as soon as words like "humanity," "history," "social situation," etc., are used. For these words are supposed to relate to the whole of human history, and therefore, insofar as this is the case, are not themselves bound to any given historical moment.

Thus it is certainly not necessary to posit an eternal human nature; but it *is* necessary to understand humanity, living in encounter and in history, as a unity, since otherwise nothing at all could be asserted, even about the most concrete historical phenomenon. Most significantly, every norm would thereby be invalidated. The passion with which representatives of this professedly radical historical form of thinking make value judgments—for example, about capitalism—and indeed interpret and evaluate the whole of human history as a history of class struggles, shows that they are by no means lacking in awareness of the normative dimension. On the contrary, they have a vision of human society in which human being will find a better fulfillment than it does at present. Thereby, however, they affirm willy-nilly a suprahistorical element: human being as something requiring fulfillment. Our pointing to basic elements of human being therefore in no way signifies a suspension of the demand, of the human capacity to "go beyond," or of expectation. For being and fulfilled being are distinguished as origin and goal.

8. For a detailed treatment of the problem of ideology, see below, chap. 6, the section on "The Problem of Historical Materialism."

9. See especially Troeltsch's essay, "Was heist 'Wesen des Christentums'?" *GW*, 2, pp. 386 ff. [Engl. trans., "What Does 'Essence of Christianity' Mean?" in Troeltsch, *Essays on Theology and Religion*, ed. and trans. Robert Morgan and Michael Pye (London: Duckworth, and Boston: Beacon, 1976)].

10. Compare my development of the notion of a Protestant principle in the following works: *Religiöse Verwirklichung* (Berlin, 1930) [selected chapters trans. James Luther Adams in *The Protestant Era* (Chicago: University of Chicago Press, 1948) and elsewhere]; *Protestantisches Prinzip und proletarische Situation* (Bonn, 1931) ["The Protestant Principle and the Proletarian Situation," *The Protestant Era*, chap. 11]; *Der Protestantismus als Kritik und Gestaltung: Zweites Buch des Kairos-Kreises* (Darmstadt, 1929) [title essay trans. James Luther Adams and Victor Nuovo, "Protestantism as a Critical and Creative Principle," in Tillich, *Political Expectation* (New York: Harper & Row, 1971), pp. 10–39].

**PART ONE: Political Romanticism,
Its Principle, and Its Contradiction**

1. Cf. the studies of the phenomenon of anxiety by Heidegger, Freud, and Goldstein; the way in which Freud and Jung combine psychoanalysis with myth research; and the treatment of death by Heidegger and Freud.

2. Cf. the corresponding discussion in the chapter on "Lordship and Bondage" in Hegel's *Phenomenology of Mind*, B, 4, A.

3. This brief characterization of the powers of origin gives a hint of the almost unlimited vistas opened up for politically inspired research in sociology and the history of religions, research that can have great contemporary relevance.

4. Proof that pagan cults and ceremonies are thus consistently directed toward the origin cannot be provided here, though it would not be difficult to do so. "Eschatological sacraments" (Albert Schweitzer) appear only later, on the soil of religions determined by an end-expectation (Parseeism, Judaism, Christianity).

5. These remarks on the problem of space and time must suffice at this point. They proceed from many years of concern with the problems of a philosophy of history.

6. Ontology thus has the same degree of justification as does the bond of origin as such, i.e., it is justified only insofar as it has been broken by a philosophy of history. The notion of an abstract "fundamental ontology" free of any relation to history is thereby excluded.

7. On the relation of might and right, cf. my article "Das Problem der Macht," *Neue Blätter für den Sozialismus*, 1931, no. 4 [Engl. trans. by Elsa L. Talmey, "The Problem of Power," in Tillich, *The Interpretation of History* (New York: Scribner's 1936), part 3, chap. 1]. I demonstrate there that neither of these concepts can be properly developed without reference to the other. To dissolve the concept of justice into that of power is equally as impossible as to imagine a concept of justice without power. Cf. in this connection the writings of Hermann Heller [author of *Hegel und der nationale Machtstaatsgedanke in Deutschland: ein Beitrag zur politischen Geistesgeschichte Deutschlands* (Leipzig, 1921) and other works].

8. "I desire righteousness and not sacrifice."

9. On the inextricable interrelationship of creation and history, see Friedrich Gogarten's philosophy of history as presented in his book *Ich glaube an den dreieinigen Gott* (Jena, 1926). On the notion of a center of history, see my book *Religiöse Verwirklichung*, pp. 110 ff. ["Christologie und Geschichtsdeutung," trans. Elsa L. Talmey as "The Interpretation of History and the Idea of Christ," *The Interpretation of History*, part 4, chap. 2].

10. This does not exclude the fact that, especially in eastern Europe, there is such a thing as a Judaism bound to the soil, which, correspondingly, also has prominent features related to the myth of origin; nor the fact that Zionism has appeared as an effort to establish a Jewish space—even though this effort is contested by those Jewish circles that see in it a threat to Judaism's mission in world history.

11. It is from this standpoint that the writings of Hans Blüher [author of *Die Erhebung Israels gegen die christlichen Güter* (Hamburg and Berlin, 1931) and other works] and his practice of setting Christianity and Judaism in opposition to one another must be evaluated. This writer, who is not unimportant for the intellectual self-understanding of political romanticism, is in the heritage of the pagan, Gnostic opponents of the Old Testament. A Christianity such as he calls for would already have been dissolved into a set of pagan myths of origin in the second century, and would fall prey today to the national myths of origin—as the theology of the "Tannenberg Group"* demonstrates.

12. It is noteworthy that this act of breaking free has a point of departure in the world of myth itself in what can be called, if we continue to employ the symbolism of depth psychology, the "myth of the son": the divine son breaks free from the demonic father and supplants him (this is especially clear in the myth of Kronos and Zeus). Or, the divine son is sent by the father as a mediator between himself and humanity. He overcomes the demonic image of the father in human consciousness and thereby opens up access to him. By showing that the father does not intend the annihilation of humankind, he enables human beings to overcome their fear. The father, through the son, frees them from themselves and gives them the "freedom of the children of God," i.e., freedom from the law (cf. the Christology of Paul and Luther).

Hegel's doctrine of the universal godmanhood of humanity that is seen in Christ is related to this myth of the son, but he thoroughly transforms it into an autonomous philosophy. Cf. on this point the discussion of mystery religion in my "Religionsphilosophie" in Dessoir's *Lehrbuch der Philosophie* [Engl. trans. by James Luther Adams, Konrad Raiser, and Charles W. Fox in Tillich, *What is Religion?* (New York: Harper & Row, 1969), pp. 27–121].

It is understandable that the priesthood, buttressed by the anxiety

---

* "An independent political, pseudoreligious sect, whose vague *völkisch* ideology posited a Germanic deity cult in opposition to the trinitarian 'world conspiracy' of Jews, Catholics, and Freemasons" (Karl Dietrich Bracher, *The German Dictatorship* [New York: Praeger, 1970], p. 131.) Founded by World War I hero General Erich Ludendorff and named after a decisive battle in that war.—TRANS.

of the human unconscious in the face of autonomy, should repeatedly give to the son the features of the father (the Byzantine Christ), in order thus to hold consciousness fast in the bond of origin. Or, at best, it conceals the autonomous meaning of the myth of the son, treating it as esoteric knowledge. It is only in the Enlightenment that autonomy breaks through the social and spiritual bonds that have restricted it in the name of the myth of origin.

13. Cf. Hans Freyer, *Revolution von rechts* (Jena, 1931).

14. This is one reason for the split between the Conservatives and the German Nationalists, who have completely abandoned the religious character of the older conservative idea.

15. The concept of the "dynamic," by virtue of its contrast with "static," is frequently equated with "in motion" as contrasted with "at rest." Such a usage, however, practically empties it of meaning. Originally the word had, and should still retain today, the connotation of the Greek *dynamis*, i.e., the capacity to be productive, pressing toward reality. Aristotle used the word in this way, and it should again be given this meaning: the movement from a productive capacity to reality.

16. Or, the effort is made to refute this idea by painting political utopias, e.g., of an alliance with eastern Europe. Truly consistent representatives of the idea of national autarky support also the physical annihilation of the surplus portion of the population, perhaps in connection with a future war.

17. One may think of the youth movement's strong and passionate drive towards community, and of how this is shattered the moment a young person makes the transition to the functions and mechanisms of bourgeois society.

18. An illustration of how ridiculous political romanticism can make itself in its efforts to create a national tradition can be seen in the National Socialist policy on art, which seeks for German tradition in the worst periods of German cultural history, those most distant from true tradition, while rejecting as un-German, out of a petit-bourgeois hankering for peace and security, the genuine breakthrough of archaic elements in German expressionism.

19. It may be expected, however, that in the face of increasing tension between conservative and revolutionary romanticism, Protestantism will turn away from the revolutionary tendency, especially if the socialist element in National Socialism should gain a greater significance.

20. The former is true of the older orthodox and liberal groups, the latter of the so-called dialectical theology. Cf. my comments on this movement throughout my book *Religiöse Verwirklichung*, especially in the notes. Meanwhile, the dialectical school has split into several

groups, divided on political and, as a consequence, also in part on theological issues. While Karl Barth has identified himself with socialism and has attacked, also on theological grounds, the neopagan tendencies of National Socialism, Friedrich Gogarten has gone over to the conservative, class-oriented form of political romanticism and is seeking to argue this position theologically—a proof of the necessity that confronts every theology to find concrete, this-worldly expression.

21. A weariness with autonomy can be discerned in all groups and levels of society. This is one of the most significant mood-determining elements in the background of contemporary political events. It is also a root of the antiparliamentary tendency of the younger generation.

22. Spengler coined the term *fellaheenization* in his book *The Decline of the West*, a book whose significance can be judged neither by its astonishing success nor by its sudden disappearance from public consciousness. The *one* possible European future that Marx called "barbarism" is seen and etched very sharply by Spengler. The rise of a second paganism in Christian form, combined with the depopulation and pauperization of Europe through self-annihilating wars, is a possibility that is closer to us today than it was when this book was having its greatest success.

23. On "apocalyptic," cf. especially the literature of late Judaism that is so called, but also the New Testament Apocalypse and the corresponding ancient literature, as well as that of the revolutionary sects from the Middle Ages down to the present time. There is always a sense of an imminent world catastrophe, whose coming and whose characteristics are precisely described. The prophecies of the *Tatkreis* [cf. above, p. xxxvi] concerning the decline of liberalism and capitalism have the same structure, even if in scientific guise.

24. The German National party* is completely consistent in supporting a policy through which it itself as a party (together with all other parties) would be abolished, and yet would thereby become directly determinative of political decisions.

25. To be sure, it is also possible that this tension-filled constellation of factors will dissolve and that revolutionary political romanticism, with whatever groups at that point are still allied with it, will join the proletariat in a common front against capitalism and feudalism. This development would be hastened if the conservative form of political romanticism succeeded, with the help of the military and the office of the president, in occupying the position for which National

---

* *Deutschnationale Volkspartei*, the leading right-wing party in the Weimar Republic. Opposed parliamentary democracy, liberalism, pacifism, socialism; supported anti-Semitism, free enterprise, restoration of the monachy, and national autarky.—Trans.

Socialism is struggling. In favor of this possibility is the fact that the leading bourgeois circles see a better guarantee of their security in this conservative constellation than in an always somewhat suspect revolutionary mass movement which, moreover, carries the word "socialism" in its name. It is frustrating for National Socialism to see how the fruits of its efforts and initiatives are thus appropriated by a group which could only come to power through this struggle, in which it took no part. The bourgeoisie ditches the revolutionary movement in the very moment when with its help the power of socialism has been overthrown. This could now result in National Socialism's reflecting on the second half of its name and seriously undertaking anticapitalistic actions. Thereby a linkage of groups related to the origin and the proletariat would become possible, at least in principle, in the coming period of socialism. But things are too much in flux to justify having any definite expectations.

PART TWO: The Principle of Bourgeois Society and the Inner Conflict of Socialism

1. I have given a thorough exposition of the bourgeois principle in my book *Die religiöse Lage der Gegenwart* (Berlin, 1926) [Engl. trans. by H. Richard Niebuhr, *The Religious Situation*, New York: Holt and Company, 1932]. I must refer the reader to this work, since we can deal with the bourgeois principle here only in the briefest form and only with regard to its pertinence to the present argument.

2. The significance of the belief in harmony for the theoretical and practical philosophy of the period from the Renaissance down to the [First] World War has still not been sufficiently understood, nor has adequate research been devoted to it.

3. The Young Liberal Movement, to which even many socialists feel an affinity, does not acknowledge the collapse of the principle of harmony; rather, it attributes the existing disharmony to the failure to carry through this principle consistently. This overlooks the fact that the powers that have frustrated the application of the liberal principle up till now will of necessity *continue* to frustrate it, since it is not a question of forces that have intervened accidentally, which could be overcome by moral progress; rather, it is the powers of origin that characterize human being as such that have shattered the harmony.

4. Thus democracy is ground down between a conservatively oriented rural and capitalistic feudalism on the one hand, and the revolutionary middle classes and the proletariat on the other.

5. "They say 'nation' and mean 'class rule.'" The consequence is that, for example, there is no gratitude for the fact that the German Social Democratic party since the beginning of the war, and especially

since its end, took upon itself the full burden of national responsibility. Rather, the patriotic attitude of the party is criticized from above on the basis of the class struggle, and even the fact of it is obscured.

6. We cannot provide here a thorough exposition of the class-struggle situation. May I refer the reader to my essay "Klassenkampf und religiöser Sozialismus" [The Class Struggle and Religious Socialism] in my book *Religiöse Verwirklichung*. Cf. especially Eduard Heimann, *Die sittliche Idee des Klassenkampfes* (Hamburg, 1926). To understand the idea of the class struggle it is essential to grasp the following points: (1) The class struggle is *always a struggle both from above and from below*. The bourgeoisie conceals the class struggle which it wages from above by means of ideology, while the proletariat unveils it, both for itself and for its opponents. (2) The class struggle is not waged at the discretion of particular persons or groups, but rather *is essentially grounded in the structure of the capitalist economy*. There is thus no place for moralistic objections directed either to the one side or the other.

7. Cf. Werner Sombart, *Der proletarische Sozialismus* [Jena, 1924].

8. Cf. the Marxist concepts of "alienation," "dehumanization," and "objectification."

9. *The catastrophe of socialist reformism in the events of 1932* [cf. above, Introduction, note 2] should have as a basic consequence a break with the bourgeois belief in harmony and its practical political implications. This also applies especially to the labor movement and to the reformist influence it exerts on the entire movement.

10. This notion of religious socialism is the result of the work of the Berlin circle of religious socialists, among whom the *Blätter für religiösen Sozialismus* originated. It differs from the basic notion of the *Bund religiöser Sozialisten* (League of Religious Socialists), as expressed in the *Zeitschrift für Religion und Sozialismus,* in that it lets the practical connection between the church and the socialist movement fall into the background for the sake of a basic clarification of the relation of religion and socialism. It is more secular, and less interested in church affairs, than socialism within the church by nature has to be.

11. The use of such terminology in socialist discussions testifies better than almost anything else to the still unbroken belief in progress and harmony within socialism.

12. Class rule makes such an education impossible.

13. Cf. the social-psychological studies of Hendrik de Man, especially his treatment of the problem of the onset of bourgeois attitudes.

It is not possible to deal with these issues adequately in terms of a positivistic psychology of the individual or of society. The fact that socialism has an insoluble inner conflict in its interpretation of human nature is not to be equated with the fact that it has had an inadequate psychology. Positivistic psychology presupposes an interpretation of human nature that has been shaken by historical experience and the emergence of the powers of origin. Already by means of its methodological approach, it makes the person into a psychic mechanism which one (regrettably) can only manipulate, when one takes into consideration such things as, for example, the nostalgia for symbols and for a *Führer*—even if, from the standpoint of truly progressive (i.e., positivistic) reason, there is no truth in them. In this manner, however, the bourgeois interpretation of human nature remains unchanged, indeed is hardened. This is why I have reservations concerning the approach Erich Fromm uses in his essay, "Über Methode und Aufgabe einer analytischen Sozialpsychologie," *Zeitschrift für Sozialforschung*, 1 (1932), 1/2 [Engl. trans., "The Method and Functions of an Analytic Social Psychology," in Erich Fromm, *The Crisis of Psychoanalysis* (New York: Holt, Rinehart, and Winston, 1970)], where he seeks to put psychoanalysis into the service of economic materialism. The demand to "reduce" even the most sublime, most idealistic of motives to their earthly "core" of libido is bourgeois, not socialist.

14. Cf. the articles on electoral reform in *Neue Blätter für den Sozialismus*, e.g., 1930, no. 9, and on constitutional reform, e.g., 1932, no. 11.

15. Not out of conviction, but seduced by a longing for authority and feudalization—just as it was instantly ready to betray its past and its principle to National Socialism, as long as the latter appeared to guarantee to the bourgeoisie its class rule.

16. These two strata are found everywhere in bourgeois society: a rational one that serves the realization of class rule, and an irrational one that serves to protect and to conceal this rule. The first is genuine and well-founded, the second false and spurious. This accounts for the deformity of "Wilhelmian" culture.

17. The present situation compels socialism to struggle unambiguously against the reestablishment of the educational monopoly that the victorious reactionaries are striving to achieve. This is a struggle for the bourgeois principle, even though socialism transcended its abstract, egalitarian educational ideal long ago.

18. The "double standard" in morality, for example, is a typical product of this alliance. The alarm of bourgeois Europe over Russia's dispensing with Europe's hypocritical sexual morality was only in the rarest cases grounded in a genuine concern for the danger of such a step; it was almost always a matter of anxiety over the shattering of bourgeois convention.

19. But insofar as it is demagogy, it has a truly demonic character: while claiming the name "national" for groups that serve the rule of capital—thus perpetuating the splits within the nation—they would

expel from the national unity groups that set themselves against capitalism and class rule—thus fighting for the true unity of the nation. This is demonic in the most negative sense of the word.

20. The fact that an astonishing surplus in production, unlimited productive capacity, and the labor force to sustain it are available, but that supplies are destroyed, factories are shut down, and the labor force is forced to take time off, while at the same time innumerable persons are thrown into the most extreme suffering—this irrationality in the economic crisis cannot be overcome by even the most rationally compelling explanation of the crisis in the realm of thought. The rebellion against this absurdity is the strongest impetus toward rebellion against the system that created the crisis, capitalism.

21. The experience of seeing how quickly it was possible, when supported by military power, to reverse the socialist penetration of the apparatus of government, in terms both of policy and of personnel, gave the death blow to the democratic-reformist tendencies in broad circles of Social Democrats. [Cf. above, Introduction, note 2.]

PART THREE: The Principle of Socialism and the Solution of its Inner Conflict

1. Cf. in this connection the concept "dynamic mass" in my essay *Masse und Geist* [Berlin and Frankfurt am Main, 1922; reprinted in *GW*, 2, pp. 35–90].

2. This applies to Pietism as well as to the attempt of German idealism to transfer the revolutionary idea of freedom derived from the bourgeois revolution into the realm of inwardness, and thus to deprive it of its power for social change.

3. Typical of this attitude in our own time are the theological and political writings of Friedrich Gogarten: *Wider die Achtung der Autorität* (Jena, 1930) and his ethics [*Politische Ethik, Versuch einer Grundlegung* (Jena, 1932)]. These writings provide the theological ideology for the conservative form of political romanticism.

4. The concept of the prophetic that we are using here preserves the essential structure of Old Testament prophecy in its most significant aspects. It is surprising with what similarity this structure is repeated throughout history wherever the attitude of expectation is normative.

The so-called "false prophets" also appear regularly. This means not someone whose predictions don't come true, but rather someone who preaches " 'peace, peace,' when there is no peace,"* for example, in

---

* A citation from Jeremiah 6:14; but since the word *Heil*, here translated "peace," can also be used in greetings, the author may be referring obliquely

an origin-related group that expects to achieve stability and power by avoiding the demand for justice. *The proclaimers of an unqualified nationalism fall into the category of "false prophets."*

5. It is indicative of our situation that these matters, which should be self-evident, must be expressly stated. The fault lies, on the one hand, with socialists who interpret socialism in a pseudo-Marxist manner, overemphasizing the economic factor to the neglect of that which was so decisive for Marx—the human meaning of socialism. On the other hand it is the fault of the polemic of political romanticism, which in overemphasizing the political dimension has obscured the Christian valuation of the individual person. Furthermore, both sides display a marked ignorance of the nature of the prophetic element in Judaism as well as socialism.

6. For the way in which certain intellectuals whose existence is based entirely on autonomy and rationality proceed to discard autonomy by autonomous means, and reason by rational means, concepts such as snobbism or *ressentiment* are appropriate.

7. The "transcendent" that socialism criticizes and the "world behind the world" that Nietzsche fought against are products of an objectifying mentality that cannot understand the meaning of mythological symbols. But the same could be said of the stress on immanence that they deploy in opposition to these concepts. A contemporary philosophy that is prepared once again to let phenomena speak for themselves has an opportunity to inquire of reality in an unprejudiced manner just what such mythological symbols might mean.

8. It is gratifying to see that, at least in Protestant theology, the realization is dawning that bourgeois idealism is not to be valued higher, from a religious standpoint, than proletarian materialism, and that on the contrary, such idealism—functioning as an ideology and as a factory of "self-made gods"—serves to conceal the real human situation. Cf. the new and positive assessment of Feuerbach by "dialectical theology."

9. Cf. the controversy over Karl Mannheim's *Ideologie und Utopie* [Engl. trans. by Louis Wirth and Edward Shils, *Ideology and Utopia: An Introduction to the Sociology of Knowledge* (New York: Harcourt, Brace, 1936)].

10. The instinctive resistance to this challenge by many groups of socialist intellectuals and bureaucrats, in spite of their regular use of the concept of ideology, is no less vigorous than the resistance of the bourgeoisie against the exposure of bourgeois ideology.

11. This is particularly true for a certain way of prematurely setting

---

to the incessant use during the Nazi period of the salutation "Heil Hitler."— TRANS.

up "interconnections" between socialism and revolutionary romanticism, while ignoring the proletarian movement.

12. Cf. in this connection his recently discovered treatise "Nationalökonomie und Philosophie" [trans. into English under the title *Economic and Philosophical Manuscripts*; various editions]. Also the essays by Konrad Hebel and J. P. Mayer in *Neue Blätter für den Sozialismus*, 1932, no. 9.

13. The doctrine of the "true interest" of the middle classes was an expression of the false materialism that sees human interests as determined unequivocally by the quantity of income. It is true that income is a decisive factor, but it is only *one* such factor. Another consideration is the kind of income and the social situation in which it is earned. The assumption that the middle classes could perceive the interest of the proletariat directly as their own "true" interest was a piece of materialistic dogmatism.

14. Even on the soil of the conservative form of political romanticism a small group was trying to free itself from its connection with the bourgeoisie and with class domination. These are the "Popular Conservatives" [*Volkskonservativen*]. However, as its lack of political success has shown, this group does not have any real social forces behind it, and hence its significance for the socialist struggle lies only in the intellectual sphere.

15. The Fascist notion of the elite comes to mind here. This concept, however, has become unusable—not because of any inherent defects, but because of its misuse by fascism. Fascism employs this notion as a part of an uncriticized myth of origin. Thus the elite does not serve the demand for justice, but is the bearer of a bourgeois, class-based feudalism.

16. Cf. the volume edited by the present writer, *Kairos, Zur Geisteslage und Geisteswendung* (Darmstadt, 1926). [Tillich's essay "Kairos und Logos" from this symposium was published in English translation by Elsa L. Talmey in *The Interpretation of History*, part 2, chap. 2.]

17. Cf. the previously cited essay by Erich Fromm in the *Zeitschrift für Sozialforschung*, as well as the writings of Bernfeld [Siegfried Bernfeld, author of *Trieb und Tradition im Jugendalter, kulturpsychologische Studien an Tagebüchern* (Leipzig, 1931) and other works].

18. We affirm, therefore, *methodological* but reject *metaphysical* positivism. One cannot say in advance how far the process of identifying objectively determined factors can be taken. But we can surely say, however, that objectifying thought as *thought* cannot itself be something merely objective, but is an object-positing, original "synthesis."

19. Cf. my essay, "Das Problem der Macht" ["The Problem of

Power"; published in English translation by Elsa L. Talmey in Tillich, *The Interpretation of History*, part 3, chap. 1].

20. The antithesis between power and justice rests on an abstract concept of justice and a confusion of power with force. A concrete conception of justice dissolves the antithesis and makes each factor dependent on the other. In historical life the tension between power and justice remains. The universal demand for justice is raised against power that has become force. But this contradiction does not represent either true power or true justice.

21. Absolute natural law is the law that, according to the Stoic doctrine adopted by many of the church fathers, prevailed in the primal state (golden age, paradise) and that rests on the equality and freedom of every individual; this was repealed with the loss of the primal state. At present a relative natural law, at best, is valid. Cf. Troeltsch, *Werke*, vol. 1 [Engl. trans. by Olive Wyon, *The Social Teaching of the Christian Churches* (New York: Macmillan, 1931)]

22. Socialism should not abandon the churches, but engage them—not in order to use them as tools in a purely political struggle, as National Socialism has done, but in order to lead them back to their own principle. In this way, it can free the powers of origin that are preserved in them from ecclesiastical torpidity and thus let these powers flow into the socialist society.

23. Cf. the writings already cited: *Kairos, Zur Geisteslage und Geisteswendung* (Darmstadt, 1926), *Der Protestantismus als Kritik und Gestaltung* (Darmstadt, 1929), *Protestantisches Prinzip und proletarische Situation* (Bonn, 1931). [For Engl. translations see above, note 16, and Introduction, note 10.]

24. On the overcoming of these contrasts, cf. my "Religionsphilosophie" [cf. above, Part One, note 12] and *Religiöse Verwirklichung* [cf. above, Part One, note 10].

25. Concerning the freethinkers, see the relevant article in *Die Religion in Geschichte und Gegenwart*, ed. H. Gunkel and L. Zscharnack (2nd ed., Tübingen, 1928), vol. 2. Other literature is cited there.

26. It is the duty of contemporary Protestant theology to attempt this. It can do so only if it will radically orient itself to its own prophetic basis by breaking through its "priestly," conservative tendencies.

27. Its much-needed struggle against intuitionism, organicism, the discrediting of science, the glorification of "action," the suspicion of reason, etc.—all of which find great favor with intellectuals burdened with *ressentiment*—must not lead to a return to the idolatry of science. The latter belongs essentially to the bourgeois, not the socialist, age.

28. The confusion of socialist with liberal-humanist concepts of education is responsible for the conspicuous lack of a genuinely socialist educational theory. Socialism has proved educationally efficacious only

with respect to the induction of adults into the socialist movement. Its achievements on this score have been impressive. Cf. the work of Gertrud Hermes [author of *Die geistige Gestalt des marxistischen Arbeiters und die Arbeiterbildungsfrage* (Tübingen, 1926) and other works].

29. Cf. my book *Masse und Geist*, especially the section on "Masse und Bildung" [cf. above, note 1].

30. This cannot be refuted by referring to the numerous individual cases of women having attained the highest level in economic, governmental, and intellectual vocations. What is decisive is the bulk of working women in the middle classes and in the proletariat who would be glad at any time, even if it meant personal or economic sacrifices, to return to homemaking. Or at least, they would prefer to take up functions more closely related to the origin than the majority of occupations can provide.

31. There is no need to give specific references to the vast literature of complaint about the technicization and mechanization of life. It reflects a widely held point of view. What is unfortunate is that the question is never raised whether an *insufficient* economic rationalization is not the real cause of the destructive effects of technological rationalization; i.e., whether it is not "reason" as such, but rather its ineffective application vis-à-vis the centers of economic power and its suppression in the social sphere that are the roots of the evil for which reason itself is made responsible.

32. Further on the topic of this section cf. the writings of Eduard Heimann. Besides his main works, *Die soziale Theorie des Kapitalismus* [Tübingen, 1929] and *Kapitalismus und Sozialismus* (Potsdam, 1931), see especially *Die sozialistische Wirtschafts- und Arbeitsordnung* (Potsdam, 1932), in which the feasibility of our demands is demonstrated on the basis of economic theory.

33. This chapter could not have been written without the special assistance of Adolf Lowe. Cf. also his essay, "Der Sinn der Weltwirtschaftskrise," *Neue Blätter für den Sozialismus*, 1931, no. 2.

Index

179